What People Are Sa...
Love Aga...

"My friend Joan Hunter has written another must-read book for anyone who desires to love fully and freely without resistance from the past. Joan has lived this book, and both her testimonies and teaching come from a lifetime of experience. Read it, and learn from one of the best!"

—*Joshua Mills*
JoshuaMills.com
Author, *Moving in Glory Realms*

"I am blessed and excited that my friend Joan Hunter has written *Love Again, Live Again*! She provides broken-hearted people with a beautiful blueprint to rebuild their health and their lives. God did this for me and I know He will do it for you, too, as you read Joan's book."

—*Paula White*
Author, life coach

"Joan Hunter is a treasure to the body of Christ, and a pleasure to all those who are blessed to call her their friend. She has an amazing gift to express profound truth in straightforward and authentic language. She skillfully shares her personal life challenges without a hint of grief or unforgiveness. The awesome overcoming miracles she experiences are a result of her choices to agree with God's Word. In *Love Again, Live Again*, Joan lovingly invites any willing heart to recognize their personal walls of limitation and to heed God's call to step higher in Christ and refuse to waste life's sorrow! Testimonies of people delivered from trauma follow Joan's ministry everywhere she ministers. I earnestly entreat you to read *Love Again, Live Again* and choose to embrace and apply the life-changing wisdom presented in this book. I did, and it works."

—*Dr. Clarice Fluitt*
Speaker, Author, and Founder of Clarice Ministries

"Joan Hunter is a living testimony of God's grace to bring you through emotionally devastating and life-threatening situations. *Love Again, Live Again* offers valuable help hope and healing to the reader."

—*Dr. Patricia King*
PatriciaKing.com

"For years, we have watched Joan Hunter live out what she teaches in this book. We celebrate her vulnerability in sharing her life lessons. Her marriage with our friend Kelley, the amazing relationships she shares with her four beautiful daughters, their spouses, and her grandchildren, not to mention her great staff, all provide ample proving ground for the practical life coaching she presents. Joan is relational! *Love Again, Live Again* will help guide each reader through the messiness we all encounter in our relationships."

—*Dr. Dan & Linda Wilson*
Marriage Missionaries
SupernaturalMarriage.org

LOVE
AGAIN

RESTORE YOUR HEART AND REGAIN YOUR HEALTH

LIVE
AGAIN

LOVE AGAIN

RESTORE YOUR HEART AND REGAIN YOUR HEALTH

LIVE AGAIN

JOAN HUNTER

WHITAKER
HOUSE

This book is not intended to provide medical advice or to take the place of medical advice and treatment from your personal physician. Readers are advised to consult their own doctors or other qualified health professionals regarding the treatment of their medical problems. Neither the publisher nor the author takes any responsibility for any possible consequences from any treatment, action, or application of medicine, supplement, herb, or preparation to any person reading or following the information in this book. If readers are taking prescription medications, they should consult with their physicians and not take themselves off medicines to start supplementation without the proper supervision of a physician.

LOVE AGAIN, LIVE AGAIN:
Restore Your Heart and Regain Your Health

Joan Hunter Ministries
P.O. Box 777
Pinehurst, TX 77362-0777
www.joanhunter.org

ISBN: 978-1-64123-154-1
eBook ISBN: 978-1-64123-155-8
Printed in the United States of America
© 2018 Joan Hunter Ministries

Whitaker House
1030 Hunt Valley Circle
New Kensington, PA 15068
www.whitakerhouse.com

2 3 4 5 6 7 8 9 10 11 **WH** 25 24 23 22 21 20 19

CONTENTS

Foreword.. 9

Introduction 11

   1. Destroy That Wall 13

   2. Let God Fix Your Spouse.. 19

   3. Finances and Relationships... 25

   4. Guard Against Anger 39

   5. Forgive for the Sake of Your Marriage 45

   6. Your Children Belong to God First 51

   7. Break Ungodly Covenants.. 57

   8. Dealing with Immorality.. 69

   9. Where Is Your Heart?... 81

  10. Give Your Sins to Jesus... 87

  11. Commit to Keeping Your Walls Down............................. 91

  12. Unmet Expectations Revisited 97

  13. The Power of Your Words 101

  14. Hearing and Listening.. 107

  15. Restore Intimacy with God 111

16. Relationship with Man..117

17. Codependency 123

18. God Lives Within You 137

An Interview with Matt and Stephanie Sorger...........................141

About the Author..149

FOREWORD

Joan Hunter is undoubtedly one of the greatest friends I have ever known. So, to be asked to write the Foreword for *Love Again, Live Again* is a great privilege for me. I have watched Joan go through challenging circumstances since she was in high school. Now here she is, a grandmother with an outstanding ministry that has her traveling around the world. Instead of Satan wiping her out, she arose from faith to faith and strength to strength in it all. Today, she ministers out of her healings rather than out of her wounds.

Love Again, Live Again helps us understand the importance of forgiveness, and how to move forward and live. So many times, the dark things of the past hang on us and we don't even recognize them. This book helps you to identify these hurts, but most of all, it helps you to be free from those hurts.

The order of the title is excellent because love helps you to live. Without love, I don't think we live a very good life. When you read the book, let the Holy Spirit talk to you about areas of love and about areas of new life.

Love Again, Live Again applies to everyone. You can't say there are only a certain number of people this book will help. This book will help everyone, because we all need to love again. We all need to live again. We all have had walls built up from the past, present, and probably will have more of them in the future, but we see how, by the power of God's love, the future can become miraculous for us, as well as the past and the present. I encourage you to read the book. Ask the Holy Spirit to reveal your walls. Read it and pass it on, because books are missionaries. They work while you sleep.

—*Dr. Marilyn Hickey*
President and Founder, Marilyn Hickey Ministries

INTRODUCTION

In many areas of life, by parents, siblings, spouse, children, teachers, or coworkers, everyone has had their feelings hurt. Whether you realize it or not, those wounds affect your current relationships. Anyone suffering with a wounded or broken heart feels a sense of separation. Often you feel that the separation from "man" is the problem. But in reality, separation from your heavenly Father is what causes the worst pain in your mind, body, and soul.

After ministering and teaching about a "Broken Heart Syndrome" for several years, I discovered that there was an official medical diagnosis by that name. Tests have shown that the inner layers of the heart actually shred, which damages the cardiac muscle and its capacity to pump blood throughout the body. Any interruption of the electrical system imbedded in the muscle hinders the heart rhythm and can lead to death or permanent damage. Usually caused by extreme stress or trauma, which precipitates an excess of stress hormones to circulate throughout the body, the resulting chest pain can resemble a serious heart attack.

The diagnosis is made by ruling out a heart attack, which is caused by blocked or collapsed cardiac blood vessels. While stents or angioplasty can treat blocked vessels, there is no quick fix for a broken heart. Broken Heart Syndrome does not block blood vessels and it can sometimes heal within a month or so. It can be caused by an extreme stressful/traumatic situation such as the death of a loved one, divorce, severe sudden illness, injury, or extreme shock.

This book reveals how to heal your heart from those hurts. To do this, you must be set free from old relationships that prevent you from giving of yourself to those most important to you today. You will also see how these principles affect your most important relationship—your relationship with your heavenly Father.

Chapter 1

DESTROY THAT WALL

Have you ever asked yourself, *What is blocking my relationship with God? Is there anything I'm doing to block communication or intimacy with my Father?*

LEARN FROM MY STORY

Loss of intimacy with God is often caused by the same thing that causes problems with intimacy in marriage. I want to share what I have learned during my personal experiences. You are reading these words right now because God healed me in these areas. I am so excited about what God has done in my life. I am even more excited about what God has planned for my future.

After twenty-five years of marriage, I learned that my husband was being unfaithful. This horrific situation was devastating beyond words. Long story short, I was released to get a divorce. Two days after the divorce, however, I was diagnosed with breast cancer, which forced me to deal with heart issues that had developed from the intense emotional pain.

Interestingly, when I got rid of the resentment, trauma, unforgiveness, betrayal, abandonment, worry, and stress, I was also healed of breast cancer. The root of physical sickness can sometimes develop from the stress of unforgiveness. When I got free of all of the above, my body got free of cancer.

Have you been so hurt that you have built a wall of protection around yourself? These walls can be constructed from bitterness, resentment, fear, anger, strife, hatred, callousness, hardening of the heart, jealousy, unforgiveness, trauma, and stress, among many other supporting emotions that exacerbate excruciating pain.

About a year after my divorce, I ran into somebody whom I had not seen for a while.

"Hi, how are you?" He asked.

I said, "Fine."

He replied, "Well, you look like you are really doing great, except for the wall around you."

"I don't have a wall around me!" I yelled back.

At first, I wasn't sure what he was talking about. Then I realized I had built a wall around my heart, because I didn't want to be hurt ever again. I didn't know what I was going to do. I had no idea how I was going to deal with it. I pray my experiences will help you get healed and whole. My story is told in more detail in my book, *Healing the Heart*.

Someone might ask, "Can you guarantee I won't get hurt again?" Absolutely not. When you love, you open the door of your heart and choose to be emotionally vulnerable. You may indeed get hurt again. When you determine not to be hurt by constructing a wall around your heart and emotions, you also lose the ability to love or be loved.

Have you built a wall of protection around your heart? Think about your spouse. Are you close and intimate, or is there something separating you? Can you freely love your children and allow them the closeness that you long for? Do you keep even your friends at arm's length so they can't get close enough to know the real you?

Your wall can have a root or foundation left over from childhood. Each of us is the product of other people's influence. We live within a belief system taught to us by others—parents, teachers, pastors, siblings or friends. Today, we can add TV and Internet to that list.

Did a parent, teacher, or other authority figure belittle you? Were your mistakes magnified during embarrassing or demeaning moments? Were you teased by other children? Did someone post an unflattering remark on social media? I know of one poor person who discovered their picture had been posted online with the caption: "The Ugliest Person in the World!"

Today, bullying is being acknowledged more frequently than it was in the past, but old wounds can be opened again and again as other hurtful comments hit your most vulnerable spots. Memories of old wounds can pop up unexpectedly. Sometimes, the look somebody gives you does as much damage as a spoken word.

There have been many teachings on healing the emotions through the years. It seems they all emphasize one aspect or another of the healing process, but none are long-lasting or permanent. You could easily have drilled the foundation of your wall deep in the ground. Cutting off one section of your wall may help temporarily, but Jesus wants that wall completely removed. He desires that your healing be total and permanent. This revelation from God has had a powerful impact on my life, as well as in the lives of those who have heard my story.

Most people want close personal friends as well as family. You meet new people every day when you leave the safety of your home. Church can offer many opportunities for friendship. Relationships

THE BIBLE TELLS US HOW TO HEAL RELATIONSHIPS
WITH MAN AND WITH GOD. IT IS ETERNALLY
AMAZING WHAT GOD CAN DO. IF YOU NEED HEALING
FROM PAIN OR A REVELATION OF UNFORGIVENESS,
GOD HAS THE ANSWER. TAKE DOWN YOUR WALL!
NO ONE CAN LOVE YOU THE WAY GOD INTENDED
WITH THAT WALL ENCIRCLING YOUR HEART.

develop and fade throughout your formative and adult years, and they all leave their mark on you, for better or worse. Are you open to meeting and welcoming new people into your circle? Are you willing to allow others to fade from your life into their own destiny?

God uses other people to teach, to mold, and, sometimes, to rub you the wrong way. Not everyone will become a friend, but there is always that possibility. Treasure each and every experience, because those events are a preparation for God's plan for your future.

Man was created for relationship. God wanted man to be His friend and confidante. God wanted to share His dreams with Adam and his descendants. Unfortunately, man developed other ideas when the enemy entered the scene.

God never forced man to be His friend or His child. He loved us so much, He gave us the freedom to walk and talk with Him or to go our own way. Do you want to take a walk with God every day, gleaning from His wisdom and enjoying His company? Why would anyone choose to ruin such a marvelous friendship?

Of course, we all know the story of Eden and the separation that occurred. But God knew that man would have problems, so He made a way of reconciliation possible for every person through Jesus Christ. Amen!

The Bible tells us how to heal relationships with man and with God. It is eternally amazing what God can do. If you need healing from pain or a revelation of unforgiveness, God has the answer. Take down your wall! No one can love you the way God intended with that wall encircling your heart.

I had to be willing to take down my wall. I didn't want to be hurt again, but I had to be willing to open my heart and take that chance. None of us want to experience emotional or mental pain, but I chose to let down my wall anyway. I have been hurt since then, but I have forgiven again every time. I am not going to allow a wall to encircle my life, because I can't do what God has called me to do if I keep a wall around my heart and my life. I have to trust God to protect and care for me rather than doing it myself.

A wall keeps others out as well as limiting my effectiveness in the world. Behind that wall, no one can hurt me, true, but as a result, I cannot reach out to others either. If I can't touch others, God can't touch them through me. Walls hinder God's plan for my life. If I want Him to work through me, I have to be His conduit and allow Him to be my defender. The Word says He is my protector, my vindicator, my healer. I have to trust Him to be my wall of protection. Since all things work together for good, no arrows of destruction shot at me can hurt me. Instead, they will be thrown back at the enemy.

> *"No weapon formed against you shall prosper, and every tongue which rises against you in judgment you shall condemn. This is the heritage of the servants of the* LORD, *and their righteousness is from Me," says the* LORD.
>
> (Isaiah 54:17)

The negative comments and destructive actions that cause pain aren't really from the person speaking to you. Realize that the evil, hurtful words and actions are from the enemy. Granted, he may be using the mouth of a person near and dear to you. However, the weapons used by satan will steal, kill, and destroy what God wants to do in your life. If you hide behind a wall, no one but satan wins!

Once I gained that revelation, my life turned around. It was almost like I was looking down on a battlefield from above, not struggling and fighting in the midst of the battle. Are you ready to take your place in God's plan for your life? Are you ready to knock the wall down and join the fight as a warrior in His army? Are you ready to love and be loved as God intended?

Chapter 2

LET GOD FIX YOUR SPOUSE

Often the distraction and hurt comes from the people in life who are very close to you. Mothers, fathers, siblings, children, or best friends can often be the source. If you are married, the source often means your spouse.

Sometimes you can invite the hurt into your life that makes you want to build a strong wall around your heart. I hear someone saying, "Surely, not me! I don't ever do that!" Actually, you probably have, and I will explain.

UNMET EXPECTATIONS

When you enter into a relationship with another person, you expect things of them. This can be good, as it helps establish healthy boundaries. However, your expectations often stem from an image of who you want that other person to be, not from who they actually are. When you expect more from a person than they can give, you set yourself up for hurt and disappointment. This is called *unmet expectations*, which can open the door for anger.

EXPECTATIONS OFTEN STEM FROM AN IMAGE OF WHO YOU WANT THAT OTHER PERSON TO BE, NOT FROM WHO THEY ACTUALLY ARE.

Women often want a husband who is just like their loving, gentle father. Sometimes they want to rule the house like their mother did. Men have other expectations. When two people fall in love, they often ignore the differences in the beliefs and traditions they bring with them. All families are different and have their unique way of doing things. That means that in a new relationship, there are going to be areas of difference that will require compromise. No two people will always agree on everything, no matter how much they love each other. Even siblings raised in the same house don't agree on everything. Husbands and wives from different backgrounds certainly aren't going to either.

For the women reading this, whether you are currently married or have been married, I am going to ask you a question: How many of you have ever tried to "fix" your husband?

When I ask this question at a meeting, regardless of the size of the group, the answer is pretty much 100 percent, "Yes!" Every wife has tried to "fix" her husband. For some reason, women think that it is their God-given duty to do husband reclamation. Many men do this also, but generally speaking, after a few weeks of failed effort, they usually come to the realization that it is not going to happen.

This drive to fix your spouse comes from expecting them to be someone they are not. You may also expect them to do something for you that, honestly, is not in their spousal job description. Women, please realize, it's not your job to fix your husband. Men, it's not your job to fix your wife. Let God do the changing. Lay your spouse at the foot of Jesus's cross and let go.

Husbands, likewise, dwell with them with understanding, giving honor to the wife, as to the weaker vessel, and as being heirs together of the grace of life, that your prayers may not be hindered.   (1 Peter 3:7)

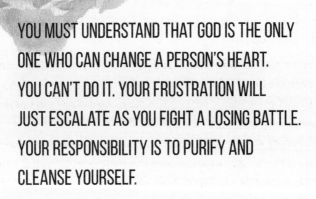

YOU MUST UNDERSTAND THAT GOD IS THE ONLY
ONE WHO CAN CHANGE A PERSON'S HEART.
YOU CAN'T DO IT. YOUR FRUSTRATION WILL
JUST ESCALATE AS YOU FIGHT A LOSING BATTLE.
YOUR RESPONSIBILITY IS TO PURIFY AND
CLEANSE YOURSELF.

Men, does there seem to be something hindering your prayers? Read 1 Peter 3:7 again. Reconsider your position and ask God what needs to be corrected.

> *Behold, how good and how pleasant it is for brethren to dwell together in unity!*   (Psalm 133:1)

Husbands and wives usually try to fix their spouses without success. By saying to your spouse, "You need to do this or you need to do that," you only stir up rebellion, whether you are the male or the female. Your spouse will tend to do the opposite of what you want them to do, because taking such orders causes irritation. The best you'll get is for them to do nothing. They'll ignore you completely. By giving your spouse to God, you give Him permission to manage the situation.

You must understand that God is the only one who can change a person's heart. You can't do it. Your frustration will just escalate as you fight a losing battle. Your responsibility is to purify and cleanse yourself. My job is to be the best mother that I know how to be, loving my children and not trying to "fix" them. As a wife, my job is to love my husband. It is not my job to fix him. I can pray for him and allow God to change him—and me, if necessary. Occasionally, my complaints (comments, requests, prayers), result in an attitude change in me rather than in my husband. That's not always fun, but it is reality.

A TESTIMONY

The message on unmet expectations has been one of the most valuable lessons that I have learned from Joan Hunter. It has greatly affected all of my relationships, but most notably, my relationship with my husband. This teaching has helped to me to reevaluate my expectations to determine whether or not they are realistic. It has also helped me to question whether or not I made my expectations known. This is still a daily challenge for me, but thanks to Joan's teaching, I am equipped to do better in this area. Here's an example:

When I was in high school, my friend's father would take her mother's car and fill it up with gas every Sunday. Her mother never had to put gas in her own car. I thought that was amazing. In my mind, that was a sign of his love for her and it became one of the things that I decided that I wanted when I got married. Oddly enough, I never expected this from my first husband, probably because, if we had a car, we only had one. We were usually in the car together so it was a non-issue.

But when I got married the second time, I was very excited that after many years of being single, I would finally have someone who would put gas in my car. Each Sunday, I would wait for my husband to volunteer to take my car and fill it up with gas. It never happened. I found myself getting upset. I started to feel like he didn't care as much about me as he said he did. This was not a major conflict but each Sunday, when he didn't do it, my feelings got hurt.

Eventually, I stopped expecting him to offer. Every now and again, when I was putting gas in my car, I would think about it. I felt sad and even a little angry. After hearing Joan's teaching, I realized that I had never expressed this expectation to my husband. If I had told him, he probably would have done it. I was getting upset because I wanted him to meet an expectation that he knew nothing about! Crazy, I know, but true.

As a child of God, you can claim His Word. Pray peace and cooperation over your relationships, your children, and your spouse. God will make the necessary changes in you and your loved ones.

Chapter 3

FINANCES AND RELATIONSHIPS

The number one argument, reason, and cause for divorce is financial problems. This includes excessive debt, but also a simple lack of communication about financial management within the marriage.

As newlyweds suddenly merge all their money and belongings together, they naively believe that everything will be forever perfect in their relationship. Then reality sets in. Rarely are they together in the same place when making financial decisions. One spouse makes a set of plans while the other spouse makes completely different plans. They each make spending decisions according to their own personal desire without the other's consent. Neither can understand how the finances suddenly dwindle down and the money is gone.

All for one and one for all sounds great, however, there needs to be specific communication on money issues and expectations. If one partner is not good at managing money, there should not be a merging of all finances until both spouses are on the same page. Having a joint checking account for household/family expenses is great, but there should be financial agreements in place, such as no

THE NUMBER ONE ARGUMENT, REASON, AND
CAUSE FOR DIVORCE IS FINANCIAL PROBLEMS. THIS
INCLUDES EXCESSIVE DEBT, BUT ALSO A SIMPLE
LACK OF COMMUNICATION ABOUT FINANCIAL
MANAGEMENT WITHIN THE MARRIAGE.

expenditures over one hundred dollars without agreement from the other partner.

Separate personal accounts can be great for general running expenses. Separate accounts are also important when there is a blended family. Without them, each parent might spend all the merged money on their own children and neglect their spouse's children. There needs to be communication, agreement and compromise to be fair all around.

Discussion about money is hard for all couples. Before marriage, both partners should come to an agreement on tithing. What do you want blessed, your net income or the gross? Agree beforehand and pray over every tithe and offering. Personally, I would rather give more money to my Father through tithes and offerings than to Uncle Sam in the form of taxes. God always comes through with His blessings. There also needs to be an agreement to save an agreed percentage of income every month for an emergency fund, future college tuition, retirement, or future purchases like a new house. In the long run, things are more affordable if paid for with cash rather than with debt-building credit cards.

CINDERELLA SYNDROME

The "Cinderella syndrome" can seriously affect some marriages. This can apply to either spouse involved. One partner has the opinion that their spouse has an endless supply of finances to take care of all their needs forever. Often, the wife truly believes her prince charming will provide all the good stuff for her pleasure, as debts mount rapidly and credit cards are quickly maxed out. This may seem strange but it happens. When one partner runs up the bills and depletes the money supply, divorce is not far behind.

Repent for foolish spending. How many things have you purchased that were forgotten in a day or so? How often have you literally wasted money on needless items that provide no sense of

PRAY FOR SUPERNATURAL WISDOM OVER
ALL YOUR FINANCIAL DECISIONS, AND FOR
SUPERNATURAL INCREASE. THANK GOD FOR ALL
HE GIVES, NOT JUST A PAYCHECK. APPRECIATE
HIS GIFTS OF LOVE, JOY, PEACE, FAMILY, FRIENDS,
CHURCH, PASTORS, AND FRIENDS. HE BRINGS
THOSE INTANGIBLE THINGS INTO YOUR LIFE AS
WELL AS THE FINANCES TO PROVIDE FOR YOUR
PHYSICAL NEEDS.

happiness or satisfaction to any part of your life? Pray for supernatural wisdom over all your financial decisions, and for supernatural increase. Thank God for all He gives, not just a paycheck.
Appreciate His gifts of love, joy, peace, family, friends, church,
pastors, and friends. He brings those intangible things into your
life as well as the finances to provide for your physical needs.

Financial philosophy can go from one extreme to another,
from Cinderella and her prince to the ashes of the fire pit of the
poorhouse. It is very important that couples agree to get and stay
totally free of spiritual poverty as well as the financial variety. Our
words can open up the windows of heaven or bolt them shut. Some
repeatedly say, "I don't have money for this or that." Those few
words scream, "I have a poverty spirit!" Such words can and will
affect the entire family. Dad says it, then Mom repeats it. Soon
the children will copy Mom and Dad. That poverty spirit multi-
plies throughout the family. Which would you rather say? "I don't
have..." or "I have everything I need. God is my supply!" Why not
add, "We will certainly consider getting that when the money is
available. If God wants us to do a certain thing, He will supply the
resources."

Negative words about finances can make or break a marriage,
or at least make marriage very uncomfortable. Choose positive
words with a positive attitude about a positive wonderful Father,
Son, and Holy Spirit, who supply God's children with everything
they need to fulfill their destiny.

THE SPIRIT OF POVERTY

In my book *Healing the Heart*, I told the story about my problem with overeating when I was not feeling good. My mother was
born into a poor family and had been deprived many "luxuries"
that most families take for granted. Because of this, she developed a damaging poverty spirit. At some point, she made herself a
promise: "When I get older and have money, I am going to have a

hot fudge sundae with walnuts every day of my life." Even though we did scrounge for good food to eat during the early years of my childhood, my mom did get a good job and became successful. Sure enough, while growing up, I remember how my mom had to have a hot fudge sundae every day, just to prove to herself that she was not poor. She fulfilled this promise to herself and enjoyed her ice cream treat each and every day. Even the night before she died, she had to have one last hot fudge sundae with sugar-free ice cream, diet syrup, and walnuts, to prove she still was not poor. Unfortunately, her poverty spirit also affected me.

While growing up, whenever I was a good girl, I was given a hot fudge sundae every day. I quickly associated "being good" with a delicious reward of ice cream covered with hot fudge. Did it satisfy me? Not really. But I worked hard to get my next delicious reward. Each reward just made me bigger and bigger.

When my marriage ended in 1999, I felt terrible about myself and my weight. Instead of reaching for healthy foods, I was drawn to the refrigerator and reached for the ice cream. I made myself a delicious hot fudge sundae way too often. You cannot imagine how good those sundaes tasted. I can still make a mean hot fudge sundae.

One day, after separating from my husband, I went to the refrigerator again and pulled out each ingredient. I was excited as I carefully constructed one more monstrous delicious hot fudge sundae. I delighted myself with each heaping spoonful. Actually, I was mulling the ice cream and fudge around in my mouth instead of just eating and swallowing my beautiful creation. Suddenly, I thought, *Why am I eating this again?* I realized that I was eating it in an attempt to make myself feel better. In truth, all I was doing was making myself fatter, which, in turn, made me feel worse, not better about myself.

Instead of bringing peace and joy, this "reward" was bringing more stress and trauma into my life. I was the brunt of negative comments and rejection instead of the loving acceptance I desperately needed from my spouse. I was adding to my problems, not finding a lasting solution.

When I received this revelation, I seriously prayed about it. I made the hard but healthier decision to stop indulging my cravings for hot fudge sundaes. I haven't had more than one hot fudge sundae a year since that time. I am no longer driven to eat an ice cream sundae to make myself feel better about myself. I am a child of the King. I know who I am. I don't need an ice cream reward any longer. I have my Jesus!

One night, my present husband Kelley and I went to a beautiful banquet. Three elegantly dressed ladies sat across from us at our table. There was one chair empty. One of these ladies ate her salad and the salad from the empty place setting. Then she asked the waiter for another salad. When the buffet opened, we went to fill our plates. This same lady piled food on her plate and carried it back to the table. She ate every morsel and went back for more. This relatively small human being ate and ate and ate. When the desserts were available, she brought back five different plates of dessert and ate every one of them. She continued to look around for additional food. I truly could not understand where she was putting this massive amount of food. I still don't know if that woman was very hungry or poor, but she was certainly desperate for food. Perhaps, she had also grown up with a poverty spirit that drove her to gorge herself with any available food. She acted as though she didn't know where her next meal was coming from.

Years ago, my aunt would call and ask for money from my mom and dad. They would scrimp and save in order to send her five hundred dollars every once in a while. They wanted to make sure my aunt would not go hungry. When my aunt died, her bank account had a half-million dollars in it. My parents were not happy when they discovered that she would spend about fifty dollars of their gifts on food and then stash the rest in the bank. They had not intended to pad her savings account.

My aunt was filled with fear that she wouldn't have the money to meet her needs. Her poverty spirit was obvious. She had never recovered from her early years of trauma from living through the depression when food was scarce.

FINANCES, A TESTIMONY

I grew up with very loving and supportive parents but they were not perfect. My father was a happy and functional alcoholic. In time, this caused me to feel insecure and fearful. Because of my father's alcohol struggles, my parents did not know how to manage their finances. They lived paycheck to paycheck. When money was good, they were lavish givers and spenders, which later created problems when the bills had to be paid. I had no concept of what it meant to save money or have a healthy and wise relationship with money.

My husband, on the other hand, grew up in a completely opposite style. His parents—mainly his mother, who was an accountant—knew the value of a hard-earned dollar. She knew the importance of saving money for a rainy day and always had enough to pay bills on time. My husband was taught to handle his money in a wise and mature way, even at a young age.

When we got married, my husband just assumed that since his mother handled the finances in his home while he was growing up that I would handle them also. Little did he know that I had no clue how to handle money, other than spend it. We struggled for many years because he couldn't understand why we never had money, or why we never had savings. It took us years to realize that God had gifted and appointed him with handling the finances.

I also realized that because I had so many insecurities growing up, I had developed a controlling spirit that caused much strife in our marriage. I had no self-control when it came to money. I manipulated my husband on many occasions to make many unnecessary purchases. I would repent and ask for forgiveness, and yet the cycle continued.

I soon realized that I needed my heart to be healed, first and foremost. When I finally decided to surrender my will to the Lord and to trust my husband (the head of our home) to take full responsibility in making the tough decisions in our finances, things began to turn around.

Then I read Supernatural Provision by Joan Hunter. This just continued the healing process in our finances as I learned that God wants our finances to be healed. Hallelujah for the spirit of truth that set us free. —S.A.

Throughout the ages, our enemy has utilized the power of covenants made with a religious spirit to keep believers apart from God's blessings. We have all heard church folk say that we should be poor like Jesus was. Sorry, that is not true. Jesus was not poor. God arranged for wealthy wise men to travel many miles to bring expensive treasures to Mary and Joseph. God knew beforehand what they needed to protect, nurture, and educate His Son. He didn't leave them stranded in the desert.

To fulfill His purpose on earth, Jesus allowed Himself to be stripped of everything. He took our sickness, our poverty, and all our sin so we could walk in health, prosperity and eternal life with Him. God wants His Word to be spread around the world. He certainly knows of the finances required to accomplish His will. He will never tell you to do something without supplying what is

WE HAVE ALL HEARD CHURCH FOLK SAY THAT
WE SHOULD BE POOR LIKE JESUS WAS. SORRY,
THAT IS NOT TRUE. JESUS WAS NOT POOR. GOD
ARRANGED FOR WEALTHY WISE MEN TO TRAVEL
MANY MILES TO BRING EXPENSIVE TREASURES
TO MARY AND JOSEPH. GOD KNEW BEFOREHAND
WHAT THEY NEEDED TO PROTECT, NURTURE,
AND EDUCATE HIS SON. HE DIDN'T LEAVE THEM
STRANDED IN THE DESERT.

needed to do it. No, Jesus was not poor. And you aren't either. You must simply learn the combination to enter His vault of riches and claim what is yours.

Break the connection with the religious spirit of poverty. Don't be lazy, or poverty will take over. Poverty is from the enemy, not a blessing or calling from your Father. God gives you riches when He trusts you to do His will. However, never trust in riches alone. You must place all trust and faith on the One who provides the wealth of the world.

Get rid of that ugly poverty spirit! You have been listening to the enemy. He doesn't want you to invest in God's kingdom or to walk in prosperity! Repent of poor stewardship from the past.

For God gives wisdom and knowledge and joy to a man who is good in His sight; but to the sinner He gives the work of gathering and collecting, that he may give to him who is good before God. This also is vanity and grasping for the wind.
(Ecclesiastes 2:26)

That poor stewardship of previous finances can be held against you proving that you don't qualify for the transfer of wealth. For instance, the golden calf of Exodus was made out of the Egyptian gold that was intended for God's use. Instead, the rebellious Israelites created an idol that subsequently had to be destroyed. (See Exodus 32.) Don't rob God. Be a good steward of all God's gifts and prosperity. Obey Him and He will always bless you with more in order to accomplish His will in your life.

Let the sinner gather and collect wealth. You stay within God's good graces, gathering His wisdom, knowledge, and joy. Open your arms and your bank account. Joyfully, welcome God's blessings as they run to overtake you.

Wake up! Don't believe or listen to the enemy. Search for God's truth. Covenants from your ancestors are passed down

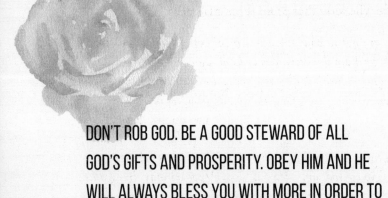

DON'T ROB GOD. BE A GOOD STEWARD OF ALL
GOD'S GIFTS AND PROSPERITY. OBEY HIM AND HE
WILL ALWAYS BLESS YOU WITH MORE IN ORDER TO
ACCOMPLISH HIS WILL IN YOUR LIFE.

through bloodlines and can affect you and your family today. These include covenants like the religious spirit and the poverty spirit we have already discussed. Do you recall stories about your ancestors revealing their exploits?

The word *covenant* usually brings up positive thoughts of "promise" and "agreement." Yes, it indicates both, however, many covenants throughout the ages are not positive ones. Do you remember the verse that promises punishment?

> You are not to bow down in worship of any images of other gods, for I am the Eternal your God. I am jealous for worship, bringing punishment on you and your children to come, even down to your great-grandchildren, to whoever hates Me.
> (Deuteronomy 5:9 VOICE)

> You must not worship or serve any idol. This is because I, the Lord your God, am a jealous God. A person may sin against me and hate me. I will punish his children, even his grandchildren and great-grandchildren. (Deuteronomy 5:9 ICB)

> You must not bow down to them or worship them, for I, the LORD your God, am a jealous God who will not tolerate your affection for any other gods. I lay the sins of the parents upon their children; the entire family is affected—even children in the third and fourth generations of those who reject me.
> (Exodus 20:5 NLT)

What you choose to do today will affect future generations. Your responsibility to your offspring doesn't end when they leave home at eighteen years of age. The covenants made by your ancestors are passed on to your children. You may not even know what they were. They could be positive covenants with God or demonic covenants (promises) made to the devil.

A man I worked with years ago had been promised to the devil before he was born. His mother had had problems carrying a baby to term. She made the covenant with the devil and delivered a healthy boy child. He didn't understand all the battles he faced throughout his life. There was a constant attack on whatever he did that was good and positive. His full story would cause your hair to stand on end! He was forty years old before someone recognized the cause and he was delivered from the ancestral covenant his mother had made.

The enemy uses your trust in the flesh—the things you can see and accomplish for yourself. This mentality cuts out your need for God. If you don't need God's assistance with something you are doing, chances are it is not an assignment from Him. He will never leave you stranded to do something without His assistance through His Holy Spirit. Chances are good that you have missed many marvelous opportunities to partner with Him and utilize His great ideas!

A works mentality (insisting on independence) will never outshine trust and faith in the goodness of God. Whatever you do, pass it through the lens of His Word. If it doesn't agree with His instruction, turn aside. Serve Him. Do what is right in His eyes.

Chapter 4

GUARD AGAINST ANGER

Many times, anger can enter through unmet expectations. There's a story I like to share about this because it happens so often in so many homes. Our home is blessed because we do not have this issue, but I've found that it is a common situation.

Who is responsible to take out the trash?

One big reason this is not an issue in our house is that my trash gets emptied every day in the hotel rooms where I stay! If the garbage builds up at home while I am gone, I am not there to gripe, complain, take it out, or ask my husband to take it out, either. I actually empty the trash at home quite often and have no problem doing it.

In most women's opinion, taking out the trash is the man's job. You get married and now you just assume that your husband's job is making sure no trash is in the house. I sometimes wonder who took out the trash before you got married. If you took it out before you got married, why can't you take it out after you get married?

ANGER ENTERS A MARRIAGE THROUGH UNMET
EXPECTATIONS.... THE WORD OF GOD SAYS, *"IN
YOUR ANGER DO NOT SIN"* (EPHESIANS 4:26 NIV).
IT DOESN'T SAY, "DO NOT GET ANGRY."
EVEN JESUS GOT ANGRY. HOWEVER, IF YOU
DO GET ANGRY, DON'T SIN.

I personally don't feel that taking out the trash is worth a divorce, but I've found that it is a major problem in many households around the globe. If my husband didn't take it out, I would simply say, "Honey, please take out the trash." Some women will allow it to sit there and overflow, as if dealing with it is beneath them. *After all*, they think, *it is the husband's job.* The husband often takes out the trash just to avoid an argument. The wife uses anger to manipulate her husband to do what she wants him to do, but no one is happy in this situation.

Anger enters a marriage through unmet expectations. A husband doesn't take out the trash as often as his wife thinks he should, so she gets mad at him. The Word of God says, *"In your anger do not sin"* (Ephesians 4:26 NIV). It doesn't say, "Do not get angry." Even Jesus got angry. However, if you do get angry, don't sin. Don't be yelling and screaming and want to beat him up because he is not taking out the trash. That's when the anger becomes sin. You need to be careful with such situations.

> *If you are angry, do not let it become sin. Get over your anger before the day is finished. Do not let the devil start working in your life.* (Ephesians 4:26–27 NLV)

There is such a thing as righteous anger, but you don't express it by yelling, screaming, and pitching a fit. You give it to God. Unrestrained anger can cause many problems in your home and produce stress in your body that can make you sick.

According to a 2012 study published in the *Journal of the American Medical Association*, 60 to 80 percent of people who visit their primary care doctors do so because of stress-related illnesses.[1] That can be from stress in the home, stress on the job, or stress about finances, among other things. If you are stressed out at work, you can easily drag that stress into your personal life

---

1. https://jamanetwork.com/journals/jamainternalmedicine/fullarticle/1392494 (accessed June 15, 2018).

DON'T GET MAD AT A SITUATION AND THEN TAKE YOUR FRUSTRATION OUT ON SOMEONE ELSE. TOO OFTEN, FAMILY MEMBERS GET THE BRUNT OF THE BAD MOOD OR ANGER. YOUR FAMILY WAS GIVEN TO YOU TO LOVE AND NURTURE, NOT TO YELL AND SCREAM AT.

and relationships. Extra stress is not what you need in your home. Interpersonal issues within the family cause enough stress as it is. You must learn how to control and manage stress constructively by giving those issues to God.

Anger can be, and often is, a form of selfishness. Someone didn't do things your way. They were laughing and happy while you were miserable. How dare they be so happy when you are upset! Someone parked their car too close to yours and you didn't like it. Is it really a reason to explode and make others around you miserable also?

You purchased a car for more money than your budget allowed, and now you complain about not having enough money to spend on other pleasures. It wasn't anyone else's fault. Accept the responsibility. You made a decision with the information you had at the time. You did the best you could. Analyze what happened and determine not to repeat the same action again. Did someone else get the promotion you wanted? God simply closed that door and has something better waiting for you!

Don't get mad at a situation and then take your frustration out on someone else. Too often, family members get the brunt of the bad mood or anger. Your family was given to you to love and nurture, not to yell and scream at.

Don't fall into the pecking order trap! This means the top person yells at the next person under them, who then yells at the next, who then yells at the next...until the last person on the list yells at their dog or puts their fist through a wall. It happens all the time in humans and animals. The stronger exert their power over the weak.

If you look to yourself for answers and place your faith in your own abilities and the world's sources of supply, you are leaving God and His promises out of the equation. The "old man" always blames someone else for his mistakes. It is *always* someone else's fault. The "new man born of Christ" knows better. The next time you feel anger and frustration rising, ask yourself,

Did I ask for God's wisdom and assistance in making this decision?

Is my behavior showing God's love?

Am I walking in the love of the Spirit?

Discover a safe outlet for your frustration and anger. Some people use physical activities, like running, boxing, or other exercises, to work off the pent-up energy that develops with stress. Others may play the piano or beat on drums. Quiet methods include writing down thoughts and then tearing them up before anyone else sees them.

Find a constructive outlet that positively releases stress without hurting anyone else. Yes, prayer and giving the problem to God is good, but, you may need to "do" something also. Often, we have heard the comment, "Go take a walk and come back when you have cooled down!" Maybe that is how "power walking" started.

Find something you can utilize regularly. Don't let stress build up from one day to the next. If it does, one day there will be an unintended explosion that can damage someone you really care about. Go to God! Ask for His advice! Don't reach for the TV controller and seek answers from the world!

Chapter 5

FORGIVE FOR THE SAKE OF YOUR MARRIAGE

Allow me to get specific about what happens when anger and hurt enter into a couple's relationship. If my husband, Kelley, were to hurt me by failing to meet my expectations, or in any other way, I would respond by withdrawing part of my heart. After all, he hurt me and I don't want my heart to experience that again. If he hurts me again on another occasion, I might withdraw more of my heart. This scenario gets repeated over and over again.

Thank God, this is not what really happens in my home, because we have learned the principles that I am teaching you now. However, for the sake of this example, if this pattern continued, eventually, there would be little left in our relationship except pain. The wounds would cause me to protect myself by building a wall, withdrawing more of my heart, and pulling away from my husband—all to keep from being hurt again.

Left unattended, this cycle would continue, on and on. He hurts me. I hurt him. Soon, the relationship is severely damaged. Our conversations would be brief and our closeness would dissolve into hurtful separation. Intimacy would dwindle as we become strangers living in the same house. My heart would not belong to him, because I would hide it behind a wall of protection.

You can easily see how this cycle works to destroy marriages. The separation becomes wider and wider until there is no intimacy or connection left. The wife goes one way; the husband goes another. It's not fair to either the husband or wife if their spouse doesn't love them with all of their heart. This cycle is a weapon of the enemy to destroy the strong connection between husband and wife. It breaks up families and damages every involved member of the family.

What do you do with all the hurt or offense you have suffered from your spouse? Do you keep a mental log of the date and time of all the blows to your ego, your heart, or your body? Can you repeat the details of your list time after time dredging up the pain and memory, again and again? Or are you following the fruit of the spirit?

> But the fruit of the Spirit is love, joy, peace, longsuffering, kindness, goodness, faithfulness, gentleness, self-control.
>
> (Galatians 5:22–23)

What is the main element in a successful marriage? One word: *forgiveness*. You have to forgive and forgive and forgive again, and then forget it! The enemy may drag up a subject, time and again, as he whispers it in your ear. Don't listen to him. He wants your marriage to fail. You want it to be healthy and whole.

If you are reading this book, you are human, which means that, like me, you are not perfect. I would be the first to admit that about myself. You aren't a perfect wife or husband. If you aren't perfect, how can you expect your spouse to be perfect? Neither party in any relationship can meet every expectation every time.

When you have unmet expectations in any relationship, anger enters. Words or actions hurt you, and you have to recognize and deal with unforgiveness before there is permanent damage. If you've ever heard me speak before, you've probably heard me say, "Unforgiveness is a poison that we drink hoping that the other person will get sick."

Unforgiveness eats at you and will destroy your relationship. The enemy wants to destroy your marriage. He will give you a thousand reasons to hang on to bitterness, resentment, and anger. You must learn about and practice forgiveness. It's not always easy, but it is always necessary to reconcile any relationship.

> *And whenever you stand praying, if you have anything against anyone, forgive him, that your Father in heaven may also forgive you your trespasses.*   (Mark 11:25)

> *Get rid of all bitterness, rage, anger, harsh words, and slander, as well as all types of malicious behavior. Instead, be kind to each other, tenderhearted, forgiving one another, just as God through Christ has forgiven you.* (Ephesians 4:31–32 NLT)

Give your spouse to God. I'll lead you in a prayer to do just that. I am going to have the men say it with me first. Just pray this out loud:

> Father, I lay my wife on the altar. I can't fix her. God, You know I've tried, but I lay her on Your altar and I release her to You. I thank You for her. I ask You to help me become the husband she needs and the man that You want me to be. In Jesus's name, Amen.

And now it's time for the women. Just say (out loud):

> Father, I lay my husband on the altar. I release him to You. Lord, You know I can't fix him. And You know how I have tried and tried and tried. I give him to You, because I know only You can fix him. I release him to You and I lay

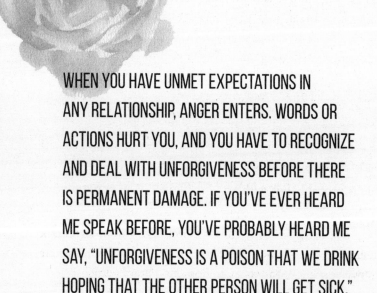

WHEN YOU HAVE UNMET EXPECTATIONS IN ANY RELATIONSHIP, ANGER ENTERS. WORDS OR ACTIONS HURT YOU, AND YOU HAVE TO RECOGNIZE AND DEAL WITH UNFORGIVENESS BEFORE THERE IS PERMANENT DAMAGE. IF YOU'VE EVER HEARD ME SPEAK BEFORE, YOU'VE PROBABLY HEARD ME SAY, "UNFORGIVENESS IS A POISON THAT WE DRINK HOPING THAT THE OTHER PERSON WILL GET SICK."

him on Your altar. Father, I thank You for him. I ask You to bless him. Show me how to be the wife he needs and the woman that You want me to be. In Jesus's name, Amen.

Now pray this together with your spouse, if possible (alone if it's not possible):

Father, bless our marriage! Amen!

Don't think saying this prayer once will be enough. You may have to say it daily for a while. Maybe you will say it hourly at times, but hang on, it does work! Say it as often as necessary. You may have to say it so the enemy will shut up and stop telling you negative things about your spouse. Remind the enemy who is in control of your life and marriage.

The enemy whispers, "Your husband is never going to take the garbage out. You will have to yell at him! Go for it!"

You respond, "No, God is going to take care of the situation! I love my husband and I am not going to yell at him again!"

"He is probably out with another woman who takes out her own garbage!" he sneers.

"No," you counter. "I gave him to God, who promised to talk to my husband. In the meantime, I am going to go comb my hair and tidy up so I look good for him when he comes home!"

"Silly girl," he says, "you are deceived! He is not going to notice the garbage or you!"

You answer back, "Devil, you shut up! I prayed! God is my Father, and He always does what He says He will do! He protects me! His Spirit lives within me and guides my every step! I am not going to listen to your lies any longer!"

Next thing you know, your husband comes through the door, saying, "Honey, I'm home! You look great! Is there anything I can do to help you? Let me get the garbage out, and I'll even help you with the dishes! I love you!"

You welcome him home with a big kiss and a smile to warm his heart as the defeated enemy slithers out the back door!

Always remember: your spouse is not the enemy. Please get angry with the right foe—satan! If you feel like yelling, yell at him!

Chapter 6

YOUR CHILDREN BELONG TO GOD FIRST

Being a parent can be a daunting task. Usually, a new parent has had little if no training on how to do anything with or for a young child. Everyone learns together. Yes, there are books and videos and other advice from the world. When you put your faith and trust in the world and money, you are standing in agreement with satan. God's Word still remains the manual for living life, even how to rear a child. Prioritize His truth especially when dealing with your prized possessions, your children (physical and spiritual).

> *Behold, children are a heritage from the LORD, the fruit of the womb is a reward.* (Psalm 127:3)

God entrusts a child to parents for about eighteen years for training, education and guidance. The job description also includes preparing them to successfully survive and thrive in the world independently. Children are influenced by so many people and temptations, parents can get frustrated by their learned, unpleasant behaviors. Hopefully, the child will learn what they need and they will follow a parent's leading, but a parent has to relinquish control and cut the apron strings at some point.

All parents have dreams for their children. Another word for those dreams is *expectations*. A parent expects a child to be the best, act the best, be the most successful. Sorry, no matter how much you love your child, they are not going to be perfect. Coming from an imperfect parent in an imperfect world guarantees that a child will have problems to face. The best a parent can do is teach them how to face and/or handle their problems.

Ideally, parents will have their children in church, Sunday school and Vacation Bible School with other Christians, where their child will learn about God and how to depend on Him (and not on their imperfect parents). Children will repeat what they hear and often act the way they see others act. Parents, please be good role models and encourage healthy relationships in a Christian environment.

We all have to face reality. Children will not always do exactly as we would like. They hurt us emotionally, just as we affect them. We do the best we can and keep praying. Yes, prayer is the answer to most, if not all, problems with children. No matter where the child or parent is located, prayers easily cross thousands of miles. A prayer is spoken in the U.S., and God's answer to that parent's petition, can fly around the world to wherever the child is located.

The term "unmet expectations" is particularly important with children. You expect them to sit correctly, be respectful, courteous, and obedient. Children expect their parents to be kind, loving, gentle, protective, and to keep them happy, 24/7. Parents can't and won't meet their children's expectations all the time either. Forgiveness must be taught and practiced on all sides, along with love, patience, and kindness.

Children are given to us for a season, then we give them back to God. The age of accountability differs for each child, but the day comes when they have to answer to God first and parents second. Parents are present to protect and nurture for a short time before becoming mentors and friends. When a child matures and marries, God says they must leave their parents and become committed to their spouse. (See Mark 10:7–9.)

No parent can carry the responsibility of their children's actions, cares, or worries forever, nor should they. Parents lose direct control of their children and must learn to trust that their prayers of protection will continue to be answered. Parents, give your children back to their heavenly Father! Allow Him to continue their education.

> *Therefore I say to you, do not worry about your life, what you will eat or what you will drink; nor about your body, what you will put on. Is not life more than food and the body more than clothing? Look at the birds of the air, for they neither sow nor reap nor gather into barns; yet your heavenly Father feeds them. Are you not of more value than they?*
>
> (Matthew 6:25–26)

> *Be anxious for nothing, but in everything by prayer and supplication, with thanksgiving, let your requests be made known to God;* (Philippians 4:6)

> *Thus says the LORD,…"For I will contend with him who contends with you, and I will save your children."*
>
> (Isaiah 49:25)

God added a marvelous promise at the end of that last verse which I stand on daily. He will save our children! I like that Scripture. It is not up to me to save my children, or to direct their every step. It is up to God! He is their heavenly Father and He is in charge. When you realize that, and allow God to do His part, God will keep every promise. He does a much better job than you or I ever will.

NO PARENT CAN CARRY THE RESPONSIBILITY OF THEIR CHILDREN'S ACTIONS, CARES, OR WORRIES FOREVER, NOR SHOULD THEY. PARENTS LOSE DIRECT CONTROL OF THEIR CHILDREN AND MUST LEARN TO TRUST THAT THEIR PRAYERS OF PROTECTION WILL CONTINUE TO BE ANSWERED. PARENTS, GIVE YOUR CHILDREN BACK TO THEIR HEAVENLY FATHER! ALLOW HIM TO CONTINUE THEIR EDUCATION.

When I gave my children to God, He did an incredible job. No worries any more. I just pray and let God do His work in their lives. Just as He knew you before you were created, He also knew each child entrusted into your care. He actually loves your children more than you do. He gave His Son for them!

Young children have been known to say, "Just wait until I tell my father. He'll take care of you!" The child may refer to a big brother or mother instead of their father, but the principle is the same. The small child knows they have a protector, a friend who will stand up for them. As a child of God, you and I can make the same choice. Our "Father God" will take care of us. Plug into His Holy Spirit and allow Him to guide your mouth or your actions. How would Jesus react in a situation? The Bible instructs us to turn the other cheek. (See Matthew 5:39.) I wouldn't advise you to stand there and get beat on, but I wouldn't tell you to physically fight back either. God will handle anyone who touches you verbally, physically, emotionally, or financially.

If you mess with me, God is going to mess with you. I don't have to say anything or do anything in retribution. God will handle the situation. (See Isaiah 49:25.)

If you respect His Word, He will even manage your business! I stand on that verse often! I know that I know that when I am traveling around the world attending to His business, God is taking care of the ministry, business issues, all employees, volunteers, and family members.

Chapter 7

BREAK UNGODLY COVENANTS

Another serious area of need in the world today has to do with covenants. A *covenant* is one of the foundational truths of the Bible. It is an agreement between two parties that involves solemn promises to one another. There is no end date to a covenant; it is binding until death.

There are three covenants that God considers holy. One was established in the Old Testament, when God "cut covenant" with Abraham using an animal sacrifice. Cutting covenant between men of that day required blood to be shed and solemn vows spoken. That vow was considered valid until death. Breaking such a covenant promise had serious consequences.

When God cut covenant with Abraham, God made a promise to bless Abraham's seed forever and to claim Abraham's family as God's chosen people. God required the shedding of blood as a sign of that covenant promise. As an indication of their privileged status, all Jewish males were circumcised (another shedding of blood) on the eighth day after birth.

And God said to Abraham: "As for you, you shall keep My covenant, you and your descendants after you throughout their generations. This is My covenant which you shall keep, between Me and you and your descendants after you: every male child among you shall be circumcised; and you shall be circumcised in the flesh of your foreskins, and it shall be a sign of the covenant between Me and you. (Genesis 17:9–11)

Then [God] gave him the covenant of circumcision; and so Abraham begot Isaac and circumcised him on the eighth day. (Acts 7:8)

The Old Covenant was based on the Law, with restrictions that were impossible for man to follow. It was about external things with so many do's and don'ts. It was a form of bondage, with no end in sight. Imperfect humans couldn't keep the Law. God required man to bring frequent sacrifices to the altar in order to receive forgiveness for their failure to obey the rules.

Along with the rules and regulations of the Old Covenant, however, came the blessings God wanted for His children. He promised Abraham wonderful blessings that would bless his seed (children and grandchildren) for thousands of years. That means you and I get to enjoy whatever God promised Abraham, so long ago, as long as we love God and live in obedience to Him. (See Deuteronomy 28:1–14.)

Therefore know that the LORD your God, He is God, the faithful God who keeps covenant and mercy for a thousand generations with those who love Him and keep His commandments. (Deuteronomy 7:9)

[God] remembers His covenant forever, the word which He commanded, for a thousand generations. (Psalm 105:8)

The book of Jeremiah prophesies what the New Covenant will do, and what it will mean to God's children.

> Behold, the days are coming, says the LORD, when I will make a new covenant with the house of Israel and with the house of Judah— not according to the covenant that I made with their fathers in the day that I took them by the hand to lead them out of the land of Egypt, My covenant which they broke, though I was a husband to them, says the LORD. But this is the covenant that I will make with the house of Israel after those days, says the LORD: I will put My law in their minds, and write it on their hearts; and I will be their God, and they shall be My people. No more shall every man teach his neighbor, and every man his brother, saying, "Know the LORD," for they all shall know Me, from the least of them to the greatest of them, says the LORD. For I will forgive their iniquity, and their sin I will remember no more.   (Jeremiah 31:31–34)

The second covenant, or New Covenant, is in the New Testament of the Bible. It was established by Jesus's death. God knew that man was not able to keep the Law, so He provided a permanent sacrifice for sin—His perfect Son. This New Covenant brings freedom. It shows God's perfect love through His saving grace.

> And for this reason He is the Mediator of the new covenant, by means of death, for the redemption of the transgressions under the first covenant, that those who are called may receive the promise of the eternal inheritance.   (Hebrews 9:15)

> For this is My blood of the new covenant, which is shed for many for the remission of sins.   (Matthew 26:28)

When you become a Christian, you enter into the New Covenant with Jesus Christ. He shed His blood on the cross as the

SALVATION IS NOT A ONE-TIME EVENT OR
COMMITMENT. WHEN YOU GIVE YOUR HEART
TOTALLY TO GOD, THE FULFILLMENT OF THE
COVENANT IS A LIFETIME JOURNEY, A DAILY WALK
WITH HIM, UNTIL YOU REACH HEAVEN. FREQUENT
"SACRIFICES" ARE NO LONGER NECESSARY. WHEN
YOU MAKE A MISTAKE, YOU MERELY NEED TO ASK
HIM FOR FORGIVENESS.

ultimate sacrifice for your salvation. We are called to remember His sacrifice and covenant in the New Testament by celebrating Communion.

> And He said to them, "This is My blood of the new covenant, which is shed for many." (Mark 14:24)

> In the same manner He also took the cup after supper, saying, "This cup is the new covenant in My blood. This do, as often as you drink it, in remembrance of Me." (1 Corinthians 11:25)

With the Lord living within you, and His laws written on your heart, you have a better understanding of what He desires. Obedience is easier than trying to remember pages and pages of rules from the Old Testament. The New Covenant is a wellspring of life based on God's unending love.

Salvation is not a one-time event or commitment. When you give your heart totally to God, the fulfillment of the covenant is a lifetime journey, a daily walk with Him, until you reach heaven. Frequent "sacrifices" are no longer necessary. When you make a mistake, you merely need to ask Him for forgiveness. You receive His forgiveness through His grace and mercy following your repentance.

As a public declaration of your choice to follow Jesus, your side of the covenant is water baptism. (See Romans 6:3–4; Galatians 3:27.) Baptism is first mentioned in the New Testament. As you are immersed in water, signifying death, it represents your willingness to die to yourself. As you emerge from the water, you are raised to new life in Christ. It is an amazing and powerful experience. If you have not already done so, I strongly encourage you to be baptized by water immersion as soon as you can.

When people in other religions throughout the world claim to be Christian, the leaders of those religions don't seem to object.

WHEN YOU JOIN YOURSELF TO SOMEONE OTHER THAN YOUR SPOUSE, IT IS SIN. YOU OPEN THE DOOR FOR YOUR OWN FLESH TO BE ATTACKED BY THE ENEMY. THE FRUIT OF YOUR ACTIONS DOES NOT PRODUCE LIFE, IT BRINGS DESTRUCTION. DEMONIC THINGS THAT WERE ATTACHED TO YOUR "PARTNER" CAN NOW ATTACK YOU AS WELL.

When those people submit to water baptism, however, their old religions immediately cut them off. In some cases, according to their religious law, these new Christians risk being killed. This reflects the power of the covenant that is made with God at salvation through baptism.

In addition to these two covenants, there is another covenant that God calls holy. The third covenant is holy matrimony. When a husband and wife come together in holy matrimony, their union produces one flesh, not one soul or one spirit. The sign of the marriage covenant is sexual intercourse, when the husband and wife form a blood covenant with one another. This consummation of marriage is a covenant that God calls holy.

> "For this reason a man shall leave his father and mother and be joined to his wife, and the two shall become one flesh"; so then they are no longer two, but one flesh. Therefore what God has joined together, let not man separate.   (Mark 10:7–9)

> And He answered and said to them, "Have you not read that He who made them at the beginning 'made them male and female,' and said, 'For this reason a man shall leave his father and mother and be joined to his wife, and the two shall become one flesh'? So then, they are no longer two but one flesh. Therefore what God has joined together, let not man separate."   (Matthew 19:4–6)

Not all covenants are holy, however. Anytime two people have become one flesh, they enter into covenant with one another, whether they are married or not. An ungodly, or unholy, covenant with another person can be devastating to your life for many years. Most people do not realize they have made a covenant with someone else, and they are unaware of the consequences that develop from that covenant.

An unholy and damaging covenant occurs when a person has a close or sexual relationship with someone to whom they are not married. This relationship outside of marriage, which can be either sexual or significantly personal, creates an ungodly or unholy covenant. It is possible for one person to be in covenant with many other people, including anyone else whom their partners have ever been in covenant with. And people wonder why strange things are going on in their lives!

When you join yourself to someone other than your spouse, it is sin. You open the door for your own flesh to be attacked by the enemy. The fruit of your actions does not produce life, it brings destruction. Demonic things that were attached to your "partner" can now attack you as well. Strange thoughts, nightmares, anxiety, stress, or other symptoms that you never had problems with before may cause you great concern after an unholy encounter.

After my first marriage, people told me that I needed to break all the "soul ties" with my ex-husband. I renounced the soul ties and I felt better, however, there still seemed to be something more. A soul tie can be a symptom of a covenant, but it is not a scriptural covenant.

Soon I discovered that I had entered into a covenant with him that was still in effect, even after our divorce. I was still in covenant with an ungodly man. Everything he was involved in opened doors of oppression in me, because we were still in covenant with one another. With that revelation, I renounced the covenant. I immediately felt a million times better.

A precious lady told her story following my teaching on the marriage covenant. It shows the power carried by this union of two people.

One night, as she climbed into bed, she heard the front door quietly open and close. A few seconds later, as she lay silently in bed, her bedroom door also opened and closed. She felt someone sit on the bed, lie down, and put their arms around her, just like her ex-husband used to do. She could feel his fingers run through her hair and caress her face.

God revealed to this woman that her previous husband was thinking about her, and about the things they used to do when they were married. Their covenant was still intact, even though their divorce had been final for years. More than a thousand miles separated them, but the covenant kept them spiritually united. With this revelation in hand, she was able to renounce the covenant and be set free.

Many times, when you are ministering, the root of an issue actually may stem from a covenant a person has made through ungodly or unholy relationships in their past. When you discover such a covenant relationship within yourself, or as you minister to others, it needs to be renounced and broken as soon as possible. This does not apply only for broken relationships caused by divorce, but for any sexual relationships before or outside of marriage as well. You open yourself up to all kinds of things when relationships get deep. There are not only natural diseases but also diseases in the spirit realm that need to be broken.

Just as you cannot accept salvation for someone else, you must renounce your own unholy covenants. I do not have the authority over someone else's will. I cannot break or renounce a relationship or a covenant you have entered into with anyone else. You must renounce any covenants you made with another person. You can do so with the following prayer:

Father, I renounce the ungodly unholy covenant I made with _____. I repent of this sin in Jesus's name and I place it on the cross of Jesus. In Jesus's name, please release me from anything bad that came into my life through that covenant. Please forgive me. I confirm the covenant I have with You and my spouse.

MANY TIMES, WHEN YOU ARE MINISTERING, THE ROOT OF AN ISSUE ACTUALLY MAY STEM FROM A COVENANT A PERSON HAS MADE THROUGH UNGODLY OR UNHOLY RELATIONSHIPS IN THEIR PAST. WHEN YOU DISCOVER SUCH A COVENANT RELATIONSHIP WITHIN YOURSELF, OR AS YOU MINISTER TO OTHERS, IT NEEDS TO BE RENOUNCED AND BROKEN AS SOON AS POSSIBLE.

Thank You, Father, for Your healing and freedom. Lord, bless my marriage, in Jesus's name. Amen.

COVENANT TESTIMONY

During an ordination meeting some years ago, I started having excruciating pain around my heart. I felt like my life was being squeezed out of me. I left the meeting and searched for a ministry prayer warrior. Prayers did not loosen the stranglehold I felt around my chest. A friend drove me to the local emergency room. Tests failed to reveal a cause. However, the doctor gave me a tiny pill under my tongue that did calm the pain slightly. Because this pill only worked on a heart with a serious problem, they kept me a few days and ran lots of tests. I was too young to have this kind of chest pain. Several of the prayer warriors visited me and prayed long distance for my total healing. Everyone prayed to break the trauma off of me. Finally, they released me, because they couldn't find anything specific to treat.

When this incident occurred, I had been listening to Joan Hunter's teaching on the power of the covenant, and what ungodly covenants can do to a person. I realized I had entered into an ungodly covenant years before. When I got the revelation, this covenant was doing its best to strangle the life out of me.

While the ministry partners prayed to break that covenant, and all injury to be healed, the pain left and the squeezing sensation disappeared.

This is a perfect example of what an old ungodly covenant can do. It also shows what God can do when that covenant is broken between two people.

UNWANTED UNHOLY COVENANTS

In the case of serious abuse, such as rape or child abuse, an unholy and unwanted covenant was also created. The victim certainly didn't participate in this union willingly. Renouncing such a covenant will not do any harm. In fact, I have seen healing occur when such unholy covenants are renounced. These experiences need to be dealt with before a healthy, intimate relationship can truly develop, grow, and prosper. The victim and their parent or partner (new or old, but not the perpetrator) need to speak forgiveness over the situation.

For example, when a teenage girl is raped, the young lady is not the only one affected by the incident. Her parents may experience guilty and anger, because they feel they were unable to protect their child. Siblings and friends may not fully understand why there is a change in family behavior. Secrets are kept, depression sets in, doctor visits increase, and perhaps a psychiatrist or counselor gets involved. An unwanted pregnancy could suddenly develop.

Family dynamics are forever changed. The entire realm of relationships between this circle of people is seriously altered. It may be that everyone involved is in need of counseling in order to survive the experience. Especially in extreme circumstances like this, unforgiveness, left unattended, can destroy people's lives for years to come. If you were the victim of such abuse, renounce that unholy covenant and, as hard as it seems, speak forgiveness over the people involved. This list could include the perpetrator (abuser), as well as those whom you may blame for not protecting you, those who rejected you, and those who blamed you. Speak peace, love, joy and reconciliation over everyone involved.

If you happen to be married to the victim of rape or abuse, you also must forgive and forget. Speak love and understanding over your spouse. Help them heal and become whole.

Chapter 8

DEALING WITH IMMORALITY

Unfortunately, when discussing covenants and relationships, I must also touch on the subject of *immorality*. If anyone has had any immoral relations with another person before or after marriage, this sin must be dealt with, as well as the unholy covenant that was formed by the relationship.

I am not trying to be judgmental. It is my responsibility as an apostle to simply tell you what God says about the subject. What you do with the information is between you and God. Identifying sin and taking care of it sets you on the path to freedom, healing, and restoration.

HAVING AN AFFAIR

According to Scripture, if you even *think* about having an extramarital affair, it has the same effect as acting on that impulse. Dreaming about sex with another person, male or female, creates the same spiritual damage as actually participating in such activities. Watching or viewing any form of pornography opens the same door to sin.

For as [a man or woman] *thinks in his* [or her] *heart, so is he* [or she].   (Proverbs 23:7)

But I say to you that whoever looks at a woman to lust for her has already committed adultery with her in his heart.
                                                       (Matthew 5:28)

Or do you not know that he who is joined to a harlot is one body with her? For "the two," He says, "shall become one flesh."   (1 Corinthians 6:16)

God's Word tells us what happens. A person chooses his or her own destruction by following after fleshly desires:

But those who desire to be rich fall into temptation and a snare, and into many foolish and harmful lusts which drown men in destruction and perdition.   (1 Timothy 6:9)

Flee sexual immorality. Every sin that a man does is outside the body, but he who commits sexual immorality sins against his own body.   (1 Corinthians 6:18)

Whoever commits adultery with a woman lacks understanding; he who does so destroys his own soul.   (Proverbs 6:32)

For this is the will of God, your sanctification: that you should abstain from sexual immorality.   (1 Thessalonians 4:3)

SPIRITUAL CONSEQUENCES

The enemy has been lying to man forever. Marriage and fidelity used to be considered important. In recent years, our society has relinquished its high value on the subject of sexual morality and purity. This sin has become so common today that few people get upset when the subject is discussed. The enemy has convinced many that it is okay to do "whatever feels good."

Pornography used to be hidden in back alleys and under the bed. Today, it is available everywhere. It blatantly tempts everyone to look at what is forbidden and opens the door to sin. Remember Matthew 5:28 above: even looking at someone with lust is the same as actually acting on your fleshly impulses.

God's Word is specific. He doesn't "wink" when His children "hook up" with one another outside of the marriage covenant. The issues of adultery, fornication, and homosexuality are considered as harmful as murder. Yes, He forgives, but be warned beforehand: these actions are not His perfect will for anyone in His creation.

There are serious spiritual consequences to such behavior. Guilt, stress, lies, hate, anger, divorce, broken hearts, and even assault and murder can occur as a result. Are those the fruit of the Spirit we are to live by? No one can tell me that immoral behaviors are harmless, or even beneficial!

> Give honor to marriage, and remain faithful to one another in marriage. God will surely judge people who are immoral and those who commit adultery.   (Hebrews 13:4 NLT)

> Being filled with all unrighteousness, sexual immorality, wickedness, covetousness, maliciousness; full of envy, murder, strife, deceit, evil-mindedness; they are whisperers,...knowing the righteous judgment of God, that those who practice such things are deserving of death, not only do the same but also approve of those who practice them.   (Romans 1:29, 32)

> Jesus said, "'You shall not murder,' 'You shall not commit adultery,' 'You shall not steal,' 'You shall not bear false witness.'"   (Matthew 19:18)

UNREPENTANT ACTS OF SIN SEPARATE YOU FROM GOD. HE IS SIMPLY WAITING FOR YOU TO HUMBLY COME TO HIS THRONE AND TELL HIM YOU ARE SORRY. HE ALWAYS GIVES YOU ANOTHER CHANCE TO CHOOSE OBEDIENCE TO HIS WORD. REMEMBER, HE FORGIVES YOU OF YOUR SIN; HOWEVER, HE NEVER FORGIVES THE SIN ITSELF.

Adulterers and adulteresses! Do you not know that friendship with the world is enmity with God? Whoever therefore wants to be a friend of the world makes himself an enemy of God.
(James 4:4)

God wants you to have fun and enjoy life; however, it is best to stay within the healthy boundaries of His laws. They are not "suggestions," they are His rules and regulations. I am not trying to place judgement on anyone for their past actions; however, I want you to know the long-lasting effects of those actions. You don't want to be dragged through the muddy consequences of the immoral behavior of your previous partners when you finally marry the "love of your life."

"It was just one night" some may say. "I confessed it in church the next day."

Great, and God forgave you. But realize that you also established a covenant with the other person, a bond that is not erased by confession alone. You *must* renounce that covenant and cut it off! Such sin may be hidden from other people, but nothing is hidden from God. He sees and knows all things. His silence about your sin doesn't mean He accepts, approves, or endorses what you did in secret.

Nothing in all creation is hidden from God's sight. Everything is uncovered and laid bare before the eyes of him to whom we must give account.　　　　(Hebrews 4:13 NIV)

Unrepentant acts of sin separate you from God. He is simply waiting for you to humbly come to His throne and tell Him you are sorry. He always gives you another chance to choose obedience to His Word. Remember, He forgives you of your sin; however, He never forgives the sin itself.

In *The Message*, it says,

There's more to sex than mere skin on skin. Sex is as much spiritual mystery as physical fact. As written in Scripture, "The two become one." Since we want to become spiritually one with the Master, we must not pursue the kind of sex that avoids commitment and intimacy, leaving us more lonely than ever—the kind of sex that can never "become one." There is a sense in which sexual sins are different from all others. In sexual sin we violate the sacredness of our own bodies, these bodies that were made for God-given and God-modeled love, for "becoming one" with another. Or didn't you realize that your body is a sacred place, the place of the Holy Spirit? Don't you see that you can't live however you please, squandering what God paid such a high price for? The physical part of you is not some piece of property belonging to the spiritual part of you. God owns the whole works. So let people see God in and through your body. (1 Corinthians 6:16–20)

The immoral behavior of professed Christians is even more upsetting. Jesus lives within a Christian. Would He casually join together in physical intimacy with one person after another? As a Christian, when you do so, you are engaging Jesus in an unholy act while the enemy celebrates. Consider carefully what you do with these covenant relationships.

BREAKING SINFUL COVENANTS

Once you have repented of immorality or sexual sin, God will surely forgive you and draw you back to Him. He simply tells you what to do to stay true to Him, and how to walk in right standing with Him.

If indeed you have heard Him and have been taught by Him, as the truth is in Jesus: that you put off, concerning your former conduct, the old man which grows corrupt according to

the deceitful lusts, and be renewed in the spirit of your mind.
(Ephesians 4:21-23)

I say then: Walk in the Spirit, and you shall not fulfill the lust of the flesh. For the flesh lusts against the Spirit, and the Spirit against the flesh; and these are contrary to one another, so that you do not do the things that you wish. (Galatians 5:16-17)

Don't laugh at Jesus and at what He did for you on the cross! Do you claim you would never do that? If you know you are actively committing sexual sin (adultery or fornication), and choose to continue to do it even though you know it is wrong, you are treating Him with scorn. His sacrifice was meant to save you from your sin. Don't turn your back on the cross and mock His death.

Do you not know that your bodies are members of Christ himself? Shall I then take the members of Christ and unite them with a prostitute? Never! (1 Corinthians 6:15 NIV)

For if we sin willfully after we have received the knowledge of the truth, there no longer remains a sacrifice for sins.
(Hebrews 10:26)

Separate yourself from sin. If you hear the enemy whispering, tempting thoughts in your mind, change the subject of your thinking. Quote Scripture back to him. That's what Jesus had to do (see Matthew 4:1–11), and you can do the same. The enemy will stop! Granted, you may have to quote Scripture often for a long time, but eventually, it will drive away the enemy. Keep Christian music playing at home and in your car. Wake up to it; go to sleep to it. If necessary, sing it! The enemy hates praise and worship directed at your heavenly Father and Jesus.

Don't tell me you can't get bad thoughts out of your mind! You can! Quote His Word and He will direct your path! Sing His Word!

SEPARATE YOURSELF FROM SIN. IF YOU HEAR
THE ENEMY WHISPERING, TEMPTING THOUGHTS
IN YOUR MIND, CHANGE THE SUBJECT OF YOUR
THINKING. QUOTE SCRIPTURE BACK TO HIM. THAT'S
WHAT JESUS HAD TO DO, AND YOU CAN DO THE
SAME. THE ENEMY WILL STOP!

Blessed are those who do His commandments, that they may have the right to the tree of life, and may enter through the gates into the city. But outside are dogs and sorcerers and sexually immoral and murderers and idolaters, and whoever loves and practices a lie. (Revelation 22:14–16)

Therefore, if anyone is in Christ, he is a new creation; old things have passed away; behold, all things have become new. Now all things are of God, who has reconciled us to Himself through Jesus Christ, and has given us the ministry of reconciliation, that is, that God was in Christ reconciling the world to Himself, not imputing their trespasses to them, and has committed to us the word of reconciliation.
(2 Corinthians 5:17–19)

I want to take a moment to lead you through a prayer that will break off any covenant you may have made in the past. First, I am going to start with those of you who are divorced. We are going to break that past covenant right now. Pray this prayer out loud—it is important to let your words be a verbal declaration:

Father, I was in covenant with <u>person's name</u>, but we are no longer married. In Jesus's name, I renounce that covenant. I am no longer in covenant with that person from this day forth. In Jesus's name. Amen.

There may be some reading this who have entered into sexual covenant outside of the boundary of marriage, and that needs to be broken too. You may have questions: *Why am I dealing with this issue that I've never struggled with before? Why am I having nightmares?*

When you are still connected to another person through an unholy covenant, these types of things can happen. Renounce that covenant right now in Jesus's name. Just say out loud,

Father, I entered into an ungodly covenant with <u>person's first name</u>, and that was sin. I repent for that sin. Take that sin from me and put it on the cross of Jesus Christ, never to be remembered again. Father, bless that person, in Jesus's name. Take away anything bad that came to me through that relationship, in Jesus's name. Amen.

You will actually feel the difference. Some of you need to repeat this process more than once. <u>Ask God to remind you of everyone with whom you have an ungodly covenant that needs to be broken.</u> Using the tools and knowledge I've just given you, I encourage you to take the time to do that right now. You can find more on this subject in my books *Healing the Whole Man Handbook* and *Power to Heal*.

After you have dealt with God about your unholy covenant issues, don't forget that if you have a current partner, you have sinned against them as well. You will need to pray and ask God for the best way to communicate with your spouse and ask forgiveness. Remember, God will bring hidden things to light. (See Romans 2:16.) If you don't settle the issue with your spouse now, fear and guilt can get a foothold in your life. You will be in bondage of the fear that your "secret" will be found out. Better to handle it up front and get it out of the way. Truth always brings healing and life.

Be accountable for your future actions. That may mean your spouse or a trusted friend, mentor, or pastor. Trust will have to be renewed. God is big enough to handle the situation. Trust Him first. He brings restoration and healing.

> *Now to Him who is able to do exceedingly abundantly above all that we ask or think, according to the power that works in us.* (Ephesians 3:20)

God doesn't give us rules to stop us from enjoying life. He tells us the best way to truly enjoy this wonderful life He has blessed us with. Living within His guidelines, we are doing things His way so that He can continue to pour out His blessings from the windows of heaven.

Chapter 9

WHERE IS YOUR HEART?

During a conference, I asked a married couple to participate as an example of what God will do when He is allowed to work in marriages. I had Tim and Jackie come to the front with me to show them a couple of things. They have a great marriage and have been married almost fifteen years at the time of this writing. They had no idea what I was going to talk about or do. To begin, I just talked with them for a few minutes.

"God is going to minister to you," I said. "Jackie, what was your first boyfriend's name?"

"Jonathan," she said right away, with a smile on her face.

I said, "Wow, you answered that quickly! I want you to be honest with me and you'll see where we are going in just a little bit. Okay, Jonathon was your first boyfriend. How old were you?"

"Around eleven years old," she answered.

"In your marriage, have you ever thought about what it would be like to be married to Jonathon?"

"I'VE MET MEN WHO WISHED THEY HAD MARRIED THE OTHER WOMAN BECAUSE THEIR MIND STILL THINKS OF THEM. WELL, NUMBER ONE, THEY ARE STILL IN COVENANT WITH THAT PERSON. NUMBER TWO, THEY GAVE A PIECE OF THEIR HEART TO THAT PERSON. BREAKING THAT COVENANT ALLOWS THEM TO TAKE THEIR HEART BACK. GOD HEALS THEIR MARRIAGE BY ENABLING THEM TO GIVE 100 PERCENT OF THEIR HEARTS TO EACH OTHER."

"No."

"Have you ever wondered what it would be like to be married to a boyfriend from your past?"

"Yes."

"What was that person's name?" I asked.

"Frederick."

"Ninety percent of women wonder what it would have been like if they had married one of their old boyfriends. Understand right now, Frederick was not part of God's plan. This is the man that God had planned for you," I said, pointing to her husband, Tim.

"But where Jonathon and Frederick are concerned, you had a relationship. I am not talking about a sexual relationship, but you had a real relationship with them that was certainly personal.

"In the process of having a relationship with one boy, here came Frederick. Cool looking guy, neat looking guy. This is the guy you think about marrying one day. You fall into what the world calls 'puppy love.' You gave him a part of your heart. You loved him, and when you separated from him, he still had part of your heart.

"As life goes on, you meet several other men. You may even fall in love with one or two of them for a short time. You give each of these people part of your heart before breaking up with them. After you got married to Tim, you may think, *What if I had married Frederick or Tom or Joe?*, because something remains in your heart where they are concerned. Those memories have not gotten in the way of you and your husband loving each other in your marriage, but there is still a little bit of another guy in there somewhere."

I continued explaining to Jackie. "Girls give their hearts away more often than guys do. I have no idea how many boyfriends you have had in your life, but I am going to exaggerate. You've got

Jonathon, Frederick, Sam, George, David, and all these other guys that you flipped over. You gave each of them part of your heart.

"Then you married Tim. You didn't realize that you weren't giving Tim 100 percent of your heart. I don't know that this happened, but we are going to make sure that it will not continue from this day forward.

"I've met men who wished they had married the other woman because their mind still thinks of them. Well, number one, they are still in covenant with that person. Number two, they gave a piece of their heart to that person. Breaking that covenant allows them to take their heart back. God heals their marriage by enabling them to give 100 percent of their hearts to each other.

"Whether Frederick has any of your heart or not, just work with me on this one. We don't know for sure, but it is better to break a covenant that doesn't exist than to allow one that does exist to stick around, just because you never did anything about it. Repeat after me: 'Father, I gave Jonathon part of my heart, and it is not his to have. I take back that part of my heart. And then came Frederick, and I gave him part of my heart. I take back that part of my heart, because it's not his to have. In Jesus's name, amen.'"

Then I turned to Tim, and asked, "Do you remember one of your girlfriends?"

"Kim," he said. I asked him to repeat after me: "Father, I gave Kim part of my heart, and it is not hers to have. I take that part of my heart back. In Jesus's name, amen."

COVENANT TESTIMONY

A friend admitted she gave her heart to a gentleman named Al years ago. She loved him very much, made a covenant with him and freely gave him her heart.

She read my teaching on covenants and suddenly got the revelation. She realized she had given this man her heart and never took it back. Even after he died, she kept his clothes and would sleep with them at night. Those old clothes were all she had left.

It was awesome when she realized what had happened. She said the prayers, broke the covenant and took her heart back.

I received this message recently:

Joan, I can now say I'm completely delivered from Al. Just now, I'm listening to the same song that was playing when I received the phone call that he had been murdered, and for the first time since 1978, I didn't break down. Oh, how happy I am! My heart is healed for real. It is finished! The song is still on as I'm writing this to you. I feel as though two hundred pounds has been lifted off of me.   —SMT

Chapter 10

GIVE YOUR SINS TO JESUS

After leading Jackie and Tim in prayers to break their unholy covenants, I grabbed a box of tissues to give them a picture of what they were about to do.

"The box of tissues represents a person's sins," I said. "My hand represents the cross of Jesus Christ. Jesus is the provision that God gave us for the sin.

"In the Old Testament, lambs were sacrificed to God for the forgiveness of sin. Today, Jesus is our sacrificial lamb. That gives you a little background of what I am going to be doing next."

Turning to Tim, I asked, "Tim, be honest with me, is Jackie perfect?"

"No," he replied.

I added to his answer. "In complete honesty, none of your girlfriends were perfect, either. If they were, they would be Jesus. Jesus did not have a spouse because there wasn't a perfect woman for Him to have."

I asked Jackie, "Has Tim ever hurt you?"

"Yes," she replied.

I asked Tim, "Has she ever hurt you?"

He said, "Yes."

"Welcome to the world," I announced. "That's normal. It's not ok that you are hurting each other, but it does happen and you have to deal with it.

"I am going to give you these," I said, putting some tissues in both of their hands. Then I said to Jackie, "One tissue is for tears, just in case you need it. The other tissues represent sin. If you cry, they might be tears of joy, but either kind is fine. I am going to have you say some things about Tim. Pray this with me: 'Father, what Tim did to me was sin. It hurt me a lot, and I don't understand how he could do that if he loved me. But either way, it is sin. I ask you to separate the sin from him and put it on the cross of Jesus Christ. On the Day of Judgment, I'll hold no accusations against him. Father, bless him.'"

As she said the words "I ask you to separate the sin from him and put it on the cross," I took the tissues out of her hand that represented Tim's sins against her. I held them in my hand, representing the cross of Christ. No longer did she hold on to them. No longer did they exist in her world. They were now with Jesus on the cross, where He paid for them. They were forgiven by God.

Then I led Tim through the same prayer: "Father, Jackie has said some things to me and it hurt. That's sin. I ask that you separate that sin from her and put it on the cross. And on the Day of Judgment, I'll hold no accusations against her. Father, bless her."

Tim repeated everything I said, and again, I took the tissues that represented Jackie's sins against him and held them in my hand, representing Jesus's cross. No longer was he holding on to the ways she had hurt him. No longer did they exist in his world.

They were now carried by Jesus on the cross, and covered by His cleansing blood.

I instructed them, saying, "Now hold each other's hands. Both of you say, 'Father, bless our marriage.'"

Chapter 11

COMMIT TO KEEPING YOUR WALLS DOWN

Asking Tim and Jackie to stand with me a few more minutes, I addressed the audience and said, "If Tim hurts Jackie, she will take back part of her heart. If Jackie hurts Tim, Tim takes back part of his heart. When that happens, when they have taken back parts of their hearts, all of a sudden, they will find that they have been separated them from each other."

I had Jackie and Tim drop their hands so they were no longer touching.

"Situations will happen, they will grow further and further apart, and then they will wonder what's missing in their marriage. Why isn't the intimacy there?"

I had them take several small steps away from each other and I stood between them.

"Now, they build a wall because they don't want to endure any more pain. They are determined not to be hurt anymore, and they hide behind this wall to remain protected from pain. When they reach out to touch, they are too far apart to reach each other.

GOD WANTS ANYTHING THAT IS SEPARATING COUPLES TO DISAPPEAR. HE WANTS NOTHING TO STAND BETWEEN A HUSBAND AND WIFE. HE WANTS PURE INTIMACY WITHIN MARRIAGE. THERE IS POWER IN UNITY. WITH GOD IN THE MIDDLE, THE MARRIAGE BECOMES A THREE-STRANDED CORD THAT CANNOT EASILY BE BROKEN.

Whenever they do manage to touch, they really don't touch with any feeling."

I demonstrated this by having them try to touch each other around me. Whichever way they reached, I kept them apart. As soon as they were able to touch each other, I batted their hands away and broke them up.

Stepping away, I said to them, "Thank you. Now you can get back together. Turn to each other and say, 'Because of circumstances, I've taken back part of my heart. I choose this day to give you my whole heart.'"

As good as their relationship had been before, it was going to be a lot better from that day forward. That is what God wants. He wants anything that is separating couples to disappear. He wants nothing to stand between a husband and wife. He wants pure intimacy within marriage. There is power in unity. With God in the middle, the marriage becomes a three-stranded cord that cannot easily be broken.

> *Though one may be overpowered by another, two can withstand him. And a threefold cord is not quickly broken.*
> (Ecclesiastes 4:12)

During one meeting, a woman came to me requesting prayer for her marriage. Things were getting very confused and her husband had expressed his desire for a divorce. Neither had been unfaithful. The exact cause of the problem couldn't be identified, but something was definitely affecting their once close marriage relationship.

When I asked her about previous relationships, she explained that she had been married before, but her husband had passed away. Almost immediately, tears flowed and she began to weep. The problem became obvious. Part of her heart was buried with her dead husband. She was unable to give her whole heart to her current spouse.

We prayed. She took back that missing part of her heart. Her face lit up with a giant smile and her tears turned to joy. She left the meeting with great expectation and anticipation.

Later, she reported that when she arrived at home, her husband opened the door and said, "What happened to you? You look like a new woman!" She explained the events of the day and they rejoiced together.

She told her husband, "I didn't realize my dead husband still had part of my heart. I have taken it back, and I give you my whole heart from this day forward!"

They did not get a divorce. They remain very happily married. This prayer restored their marriage.

Covenants end with the death of a spouse. However, taking your heart back even applies to those who have died. Have you lost a spouse in the past? Pray the prayer and take back your heart so you can freely give it, 100 percent, to the special spouse God has given you, or the one He has planned for your future.

Listen to this young man's heart as he shares his experience:

I want to share a little bit about my heart and how this ministry has impacted my life. As most young people do, I fell in love with the person I planned to be with for the rest of my life. When our five-year relationship ended horribly, it felt as though my life was coming to an end. I never realized how such an experience could impact me. When you are a man, you stand up and go for it, you keep going forward, no matter what comes your way. So I hid my pain.

It wasn't until I was introduced to Joan Hunter Ministries that things changed. When I heard her teaching about taking back the pieces of your heart, I didn't realize how many pieces of my heart were missing. It was hard to believe how my heart was still in pain.

By the Spirit of God, and the guidance of Joan's teaching, God has restored my heart. The breakup happened about seven years ago. I have never pursued anybody since then. I never had it in me. Now, seven years later, I finally feel I can step out there. When the time is right, I feel I have a heart to give to somebody. It is all thanks to God and this ministry. If I got connected to this ministry for just this one thing, it will have been worth it.

If you feel parts of your heart missing, repeat this prayer:

Father, I take back every piece of my heart that I have given to anyone in the past. I choose to give You my whole heart, Father. I want 100 percent of my heart to give to the special person You have given to me, or to the one You have planned for me in the future. Thank You, Father, for showing me Your plan for my future mate! In Jesus's name. Amen!

Chapter 12

UNMET EXPECTATIONS REVISITED

Too often, excess baggage of previous broken relationships is dragged into a new relationship. It can be a difficult situation to manage. Previous experiences develop and form the people we are today. The pleasant experiences of our past provide great memories, while experiences that led to abuse, neglect, or anger create lasting feelings of hurt and caution. The walls we create may seem shallow and weak to some people, but a strong iron barrier to others.

Don't bring unmet expectations or disappointments from previous relationships into your marriage.

If you have been hurt in a relationship—as we all have at one time or another—do everything you can to get as spiritually and mentally healthy as possible before entering into another relationship. Damaged people damage others if they fail to seek help for themselves before taking that step again.

Analyze what happened in previous relationships. Were they lessons from God meant to teach you some truth? Or were they

DON'T BRING UNMET EXPECTATIONS OR DISAPPOINTMENTS FROM PREVIOUS RELATIONSHIPS INTO YOUR MARRIAGE. IF YOU HAVE BEEN HURT IN A RELATIONSHIP—AS WE ALL HAVE AT ONE TIME OR ANOTHER—DO EVERYTHING YOU CAN TO GET AS SPIRITUALLY AND MENTALLY HEALTHY AS POSSIBLE BEFORE ENTERING INTO ANOTHER RELATIONSHIP.

attacks from the enemy, trying to draw you into his lair of deceit and pain, and preventing you from fully being of service to God? Every experience we have is a learning opportunity. What have you learned? Did you rush into something that looked good but turned out to be a façade? Or did a good relationship turn ugly and spiral out of your control?

Chapter 13

THE POWER OF YOUR WORDS

What are you confessing over your heart, your spouse, and your life?

Recently, a man came forward for prayer. He felt like he was losing his mind. I asked him how long he had felt this way.

"Well," he said, "pretty much ever since the time I divorced my first wife."

I had him renounce and cut off that covenant. I told him to take back his heart. Then I asked him, "Have you ever said, 'My wife is driving me crazy?'"

He replied, "Yes, I used to say it all the time."

"Well, God was just answering your words!" I answered.

The congregation gasped. The pastor thought that revelation was awesome. Suddenly, it clicked. He was totally set free.

Thoughtfully, consider any negative words or comments you have made over your spouse or other close relationship. Renounce the covenant if you are no longer with that spouse, and then take

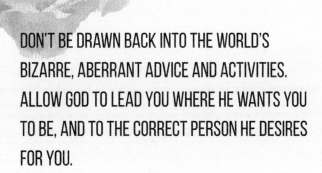

DON'T BE DRAWN BACK INTO THE WORLD'S
BIZARRE, ABERRANT ADVICE AND ACTIVITIES.
ALLOW GOD TO LEAD YOU WHERE HE WANTS YOU
TO BE, AND TO THE CORRECT PERSON HE DESIRES
FOR YOU.

back your heart. Definitely, cut off those words. Place the person on the altar and forgive them.

Is there any unforgiveness hiding in a dark corner of your heart? Drag it out into the light and get rid of it. If you don't forgive, you are hurting yourself, not the other person.

Bear with each other and forgive one another if any of you has a grievance against someone. Forgive as the Lord forgave you. And over all these virtues put on love, which binds them all together in perfect unity.   (Colossians 3:13–14 NIV)

Seek God. Read His Word. Find His healing promises. Seek Him for His plan for your life. Choose your friends well. Draw strength from other believers, teachers, and counselors. Don't be drawn back into the world's bizarre, aberrant advice and activities. Allow God to lead you where He wants you to be, and to the correct person He desires for you. Everyone needs warmth, comfort, and love, but you must allow God to choose your partner. Do not depend solely on your lonely heart.

Choose to stay sexually pure for that special person who is waiting for you. God is preparing their heart just as He is preparing yours. While you are waiting, hang on to God. Follow His direction. Spend time with Him in prayer and in His Word. Study things that will help you grow and develop in Him. Don't waste time searching the streets for a mate. Trust your mentors and pastors. Allow your spiritual leaders to meet your new friends, and listen to their counsel. Don't stay isolated.

When you meet a potential mate, meet their friends. Learn as much as possible about the other person before making any permanent commitment. Do they love God? Are they saved and as committed as you are? Do you agree on spiritual beliefs and faith in God? Do they encourage you to get closer to God or subtly draw you away?

DON'T JUDGE A NEW FRIEND BY THE FAILURES
OF THEIR PREVIOUS RELATIONSHIPS. LET
PEOPLE DEVELOP IN FRONT OF YOU. EXPECT THE
BEST AND PRAY GOD'S WILL OVER EACH AND
EVERY ENCOUNTER. BE OPEN AND WILLING TO
COMPROMISE AND LISTEN. EACH PERSON
BRINGS DIFFERENT EXPERIENCES AND BELIEFS
TO THE TABLE.

Make use of your Christian friends and family. Don't look at any close relationship through rose-colored glasses or move too quickly to give your heart away. Listen to good counsel and let God direct you. The desire to be wanted, loved, and cared for can often blind us to hidden realities that other people can clearly see.

Don't judge a new friend by the failures of their previous relationships. Let people develop in front of you. Expect the best and pray God's will over each and every encounter. Be open and willing to compromise and listen. Each person brings different experiences and beliefs to the table. Get to know each other and learn to love the differences. Celebrate the strengths and weaknesses in each other. Don't allow the enemy to destroy another relationship. Listen to God.

Some people will touch your life deeply within a short period of time. You have a divine appointment and then they may move on to other places. You may or may not ever meet them again. God directs us toward and through the lessons we are to learn to remain in His will. Don't hang on to the old when His opportunities for the new are beckoning. There are new people to meet and pray for, new lessons to learn, awesome revelations to experience, and an exciting Christian life to live. Go after God. Follow His lead. Stay in His will.

Believe that God will bring what is done in secret into the open. Pray that He will bless or block any situation you are facing right now regarding any relationship. If it is not ordered of God, you need to turn your back and run the other direction. Follow Him! Follow His peace!

What is hidden he brings forth to light.   (Job 28:11)

Chapter 14

HEARING AND LISTENING

What is the difference between hearing and listening?

Hearing is the ability to perceive sound and understand fully what is being said. To listen, you pay attention and make a conscious effort to hear something.

With all the sounds bombarding us daily, we are conditioned to ignore much of what goes on around us. It is called "selective hearing." You hear and understand only what you want to hear. There is no way to comprehend every sound or conversation that occurs within a ten- to fifteen-foot radius around you. You must consciously choose the ones that interest you and then concentrate on hearing or listening to every word or sound.

Most people can "hear" sounds from a distance, but to "listen" and "understand" the full meaning of sound is another thing indeed. A mother can hear all the kids playing outside, but she can pinpoint the cry of her own precious child through the din of all the other children. A mother may also be awakened from a sound sleep by an almost undistinguishable whimper from her baby's crib in the next room.

BOTH PARTNERS NEED TO COMMUNICATE THEIR
NEEDS AND LISTEN TO THE NEEDS OF EACH
OTHER IN ORDER TO ACHIEVE THE LEVELS OF
COMPROMISE NECESSARY FOR BASIC LOVE AND
CONSIDERATION TO FLOURISH. PAY ATTENTION
TO YOUR PARTNER'S HABITS AND NEEDS. FIND A
COMPROMISE SO EACH CAN GET WHAT THEY NEED.

LISTENING IN RELATIONSHIPS

It can happen with both partners, but it seems to occur mostly with women. They beg. "Please, hear me. Please, hear my heart!" The way a person learns to listen and react is affected by all the relationships in their past. If you asked a question once and were rebuked, the next time you may hesitate before speaking. After this happens many times, you learn to stay silent and pray.

There may be times when one partner is not trying to tell the other what to do, however, there is obviously something being done or said that makes the other person grow angry because they feel criticized or unfairly judged. That sad look in their eye may be screaming, "Please, hear my heart!"

Many couples admit they have problems with listening within their relationship. One person is talking, but the other person doesn't hear anything that is said. It is well documented that women like to communicate and describe events much more colorfully and in more detail than men do. It sometimes seems as though a man only hears every few words and feels he can sum up his sweetheart's day in one or two words.

Since there are no mandatory premarital classes on communication, most couples have to learn as they go. Men may occasionally try to express something they feel is important in a few words, expecting their wife to instantly understand all the intricate details that remain unspoken. No matter how long a couple has been together, they will never be able to read each other's minds. It takes much practice to truly communicate effectively.

Some people are at their best late in the evening and have a problem bouncing out of bed first thing in the morning. Other people are at their best in the wee early hours of the dawn before falling asleep watching the evening news. A late night of studying, a sick child, or plain old insomnia may rob one partner of their needed rest, while the other partner snoozes peacefully. The early riser may bounce out of bed; make noise, open or shut doors, talk or sing to themselves, which irritates the partner who is trying to sleep. Both partners need to communicate their needs and listen to the needs of each other in order to achieve the levels of compromise necessary for basic love and consideration to flourish. Pay attention to your partner's habits and needs. Find a compromise so each can get what they need.

If behaviors become irritating, sit down, face to face, and do your best to listen to each other—concentrate and communicate. Value the great times in the relationship, and compromise in areas that will keep strife out of the situation. Don't just "hear" noise when your partner is talking. "Listen" to what they are saying. Repeat back what you hear them saying so they feel valued and listened to.

While ministering, listen carefully to the person in need and hear the pain behind their words. You must hear the words spoken to you, but you have to carefully listen to the Holy Spirit at the same time in order to know how best to minister to a particular situation.

Pay attention to the words they use, the look in their eyes, and the way they stand and speak. Body language, hands, and the posture of the head will all speak volumes about the person before you even hear the details about their situation. If you truly want to help another person, learn to listen well. Don't just hear noise, listen to their heart, and then speak encouraging words to help them begin to heal.

Chapter 15

RESTORE INTIMACY WITH GOD

Have you ever felt that God let you down? Has He failed to act in the way that you thought He should act? Have you become upset, mad, or hurt when God didn't answer prayers the way you expected? Did you feel that your way was better than His way? Did you blame Him when someone became sick or died? Because of this, did you take back part of your heart from God?

As I write this, I imagine that you, like most people, are probably nodding in affirmation that at least one of these questions hit home. It's easy to think about unmet expectations in which a spouse is concerned, but people don't really want to acknowledge that the same problem can be affecting their relationship with God. People don't want to acknowledge that God's work can sometimes hurt their feelings, and they respond by pulling away from Him.

When you feel hurt or disappointed, you may want to take back part of your heart. This experience is not reserved only for a person who hurts you. When you have unmet expectations related to God, it's hard to put your full trust in Him, as you should. Most

WHEN YOU HAVE UNMET EXPECTATIONS RELATED TO GOD, IT'S HARD TO PUT YOUR FULL TRUST IN HIM, AS YOU SHOULD. MOST DON'T WANT TO ADMIT THAT THEY HAVE PULLED AWAY FROM GOD IN THE SAME WAY THAT THEY OFTEN PULL AWAY FROM PEOPLE. IT HAPPENS MORE THAN MOST PEOPLE WANT TO ADMIT.

don't want to admit that they have pulled away from God in the same way that they often pull away from people. It happens more than most people want to admit.

When you sit in your prayer closet to have devotions, you can say, "God, there's something wrong between us and I don't know what it is. The intimacy we used to have is not there anymore. What is blocking our relationship?"

There are two possibilities, and I'm sure you've considered the first already. First, there could be hidden and unrepented sin in your life that is keeping you distant from God. If you have repented—turned from actively sinning—and set your desire back on God, let me disarm all accusation and condemnation by saying that this is most likely not the problem between you and God. None of us is perfect. Yes, we may need to repent of sins of commission or omission on a daily basis. I, however, am referring to repetitive sins that you know are wrong, yet you do them anyway. A good example is adultery.

Second, there may be those times when you felt He let you down. Instead of going to God with your hurting heart, you back away, saying, "Why should I ask Him for a new house? He didn't give it to me last time." "Why didn't God protect me from rejection? Why didn't God protect me from abuse? Why didn't He do things my way?" You have allowed yourself to take back parts of your heart from God so you wouldn't feel hurt again. Why didn't God work out your particular situation the way you thought He should have? Often the pain in your heart may have been planted by other people's actions or words, but it can also begin when you feel that God let you down.

I could easily ask, "God, why didn't You restore my first marriage?" The answer is that God won't override a person's will. He also won't make you stop sinning. You have to make that choice yourself.

GOD KNOWS EVERYTHING YOU HAVE DONE IN THE
PAST—THE GOOD, THE BAD, AND THE UGLY.
HE KNEW YOU BEFORE YOU WERE BORN.
HE CHOSE YOUR MOTHER AND FATHER AND
ALLOWED THE PERFECT DNA TO CREATE *YOU!*
HE HAS SPECIAL PLANS FOR YOU. YOUR BEHAVIOR
AND PERSONALITY ARE NO SURPRISE TO HIM.
HE HASN'T PUT UP A BARRIER BETWEEN YOU.
YOU ARE THE ONE WHO HAS ALLOWED THE WALL
TO DEVELOP.

The truth is, God didn't let you down. He fulfilled His plans His way. I do believe that God knows best. When you insist on doing things your way, it is like saying to God, "I don't believe You know what You are doing. I am going to do things my way!" That act of rebellion will not bring positive results!

God doesn't want you to hurt. He doesn't desire pain to remain in your heart anymore. He wants you to know that He loves you unconditionally with His whole heart. He wants you to come home and enjoy that intimate relationship that you used to have, and long to have, with Him once again. He wants free access to your whole heart.

God knows everything you have done in the past—the good, the bad, and the ugly. He knew you before you were born. He chose your mother and father and allowed the perfect DNA to create *you*! He has special plans for you. Your behavior and personality are no surprise to Him. He hasn't put up a barrier between you. You are the one who has allowed the wall to develop. Break down your wall!

Whatever is in the way is blocking you from experiencing His true love for you. God misses you. He misses that relationship He used to have with you. He wants an even greater relationship with you than you can ever imagine. Choose to return to Him. Run into His welcoming arms and find His peace and love once again.

Listen to God! Listen for His voice. He speaks in many different ways. Open your heart and mind to His heart through His Word. Spend time, concentrate, and focus on Him!

God's love never wavers, but yours can. He never forgets you, neglects you, or leaves you; however, you can be guilty of ignoring and neglecting Him. Renew your holy covenant with your Father, who longs to have a wonderful, close relationship with you, the apple of His eye.

> *Nevertheless I have this against you, that you have left your first love. Remember therefore from where you have fallen; repent and do the first works, or else I will come to you quickly and remove your lampstand from its place—unless you repent.* (Revelation 2:4–5)

By hanging on to part of your heart, you are living by your own strength without God's help. Have you left your first true love—your Father? The intimacy you once felt for God began when you freely gave your heart to Him. He still wants your love and fellowship.

> *And the Scripture was fulfilled which says, "Abraham believed God, and it was accounted to him for righteousness." And he was called the friend of God.* (James 2:23)

Give God your whole heart again, and that intimacy can return once more. Pray the following out loud:

Father, I have sinned. I repent of that. Take this sin from me and put it on the cross, never to be remembered again. Father, whatever it is in my life that has been blocking my relationship with You, please reveal it to me, because I don't want anything in me that is not of You.

Through the years and disappointments, there were times I blamed You for situations. Because of this, I took back part of my heart. I choose, right now, to give you my whole heart. I don't want anything in the way of our relationship.

Father, I love You. For the rest of my life, I want to know more and more about what it means to be Your child. Guide me through Your Holy Spirit and revelation wherever I go. Father, anoint me to be used of You in a mighty way. Amen.

Chapter 16

RELATIONSHIP WITH MAN

Your relationship with God is, of course, the most important relationship in life. He should always be your first priority. Your vertical relationship with Him will affect your horizontal relationship with the world, especially with the people closest to you. Without a close relationship and communication with your heavenly Father, you will probably have problems with your spouse, the closest person to you with "skin on," as well as other family members and friends.

Your family is the first source of friendship. Mom and Dad are the protectors, mentors, and teachers for many years; however, they should also develop into good friends as you reach maturity. Your siblings should always be considered good friends. Of course, family also shares deep love and caring, which sometimes supplements deep friendship. Unfortunately, many families have deep divisions between members. Have you ever heard someone say, "I love them but I don't like them very much"?

Whether family members or friends from outside your close family circle, everyone has a choice to follow God's principles or be deceived by the enemy. Hopefully, Christian parents have instilled enough of God's Word into their kids before releasing them into society to fight the battles of life. Unfortunately, many don't have that foundation to stand on and they choose to rebel against rules and regulations.

You come into contact with all kinds of people in life. How you react to them will have a definite effect on the other person. Stand strong in God's Word with love and understanding. Choose close friends who will love you enough to speak truth, people who will encourage you and stand in agreement with you to fight the good fight of faith. Always allow God to work through your words, actions and thoughts. He does know best.

> *The righteous should choose his friends carefully, for the way of the wicked leads them astray.*   (Proverbs 12:26)

> *A man who has friends must himself be friendly, but there is a friend who sticks closer than a brother.*   (Proverbs 18:24)

> *As iron sharpens iron, so a friend sharpens a friend.*
>   (Proverbs 27:17 NLT)

Possibilities for friendships pass you by each and every day. Everyone you meet is a candidate. Some become instant friends, others are held at a distance. As you grow through childhood and mature into adulthood, thousands of people cross your path. Are they important to your development? Has God brought you two together for a purpose? Similar interests or experiences may draw you together. Pleasant conversation, introductions by a mutual friend, or a need for their specific expertise may add them to your circle of acquaintances. Eventually, new faces become old friends.

Finding fellow Christians is important. God brings people together to support and encourage one another, and to pray together in agreement. He teaches you how to stand alongside each other to fight the enemy.

No one has to stand alone. Yes, you have God standing with you at all times. But having other people standing with you is also important. It encourages both you and them.

> *Two are better than one, because they have a good return for their labor: if either of them falls down, one can help the other up. But pity anyone who falls and has no one to help them up.* (Ecclesiastes 4:9–10 NIV)

God wants you to be open and friendly to the world; but, be watchful. Your friends have an effect on you. Make sure you hang on to God and His precepts. Do not allow the enemy to creep in through an unsuspecting person who draws you away from God and His plan for your life. A friend may come into your life for a day, a season, or a lifetime. They will affect you, and you will affect them. A good friend will always help you get closer to God. What kind of friend are you?

Since the Great Commission tells us to spread the gospel throughout the world, we certainly have to communicate with other people. A grouchy, unfriendly person will certainly not attract anyone to get close. A miserable person in ragged, dirty clothes will not make anyone believe in a good God who blesses His children with good things. A smiling, happy person will! Sincere love and kindness is contagious! Let Jesus shine through your eyes and smile!

This is also important when dealing with a spouse. The enemy loves to sneak in through the weakest member of a family or marriage partnership. Weigh words and ideas against the Word of God, no matter who speaks it. You are bombarded with things of the world daily. The interactions you have with the Internet, TV, radio, media, and people on a daily basis may all have mixed messages.

MAKE SURE YOU HANG ON TO GOD AND HIS
PRECEPTS. DO NOT ALLOW THE ENEMY TO
CREEP IN THROUGH AN UNSUSPECTING PERSON
WHO DRAWS YOU AWAY FROM GOD AND HIS PLAN
FOR YOUR LIFE. A FRIEND MAY COME INTO YOUR
LIFE FOR A DAY, A SEASON, OR A LIFETIME. THEY
WILL AFFECT YOU, AND YOU WILL AFFECT THEM.
A GOOD FRIEND WILL ALWAYS HELP YOU GET
CLOSER TO GOD.

Discernment is vital. Does the person you are talking to act and speak like Jesus? Do they show and express love? If they do, you will have a warm, loving conversation and interaction. If you receive negative, ugly responses, that person is probably listening to wrong voices and is in need of warmth and love. Don't follow them down their negative path. Pull them up to touch the same Giver of life and love who saved you.

Your reaction to others will determine the atmosphere you experience. If the enemy is speaking through them, they may not immediately recognize the source. But it is important to realize the response you are receiving is from the enemy, who is actually fighting the Jesus inside of you. What would Jesus want you to do or say?

You shouldn't have to withstand any kind of abuse, however, fighting back, physically or verbally, is not the answer either. If necessary, follow Jesus's example: leave the situation quietly and pray. Let God take control.

> *Perfume and incense bring joy to the heart, and the pleasantness of a friend springs from their heartfelt advice.*
> (Proverbs 27:9 NIV)

> *Love each other with genuine affection, and take delight in honoring each other.* (Romans 12:10 NLT)

Arguments, disagreements, and violence so easily break up friendships, as well as other relationships. What is the answer? First, check yourself. Don't allow negative emotions to uncontrollably rise up within you. Pray peace over the situation and ask God for the answer. You may or may not hear Him immediately. Every event of life is a learning experience. Examine what happened and spiritually discern the cause of the disruption.

Ask the Father to forgive you if you should have handled things differently. Most important, forgive the other people involved. You have no idea what triggered an outburst. Chances are, their rage or anger didn't have anything to do with you at all. You were there at the time and received the brunt of the disturbance. You've heard the saying, "The wrong place at the wrong time." Think about it for a minute. Perhaps things would have been even worse if you weren't there. The Jesus in you may have kept the situation under control.

If you believe any encounter could become unpleasant, pray God's peace over the situation before you even arrive on the scene. You can set the atmosphere. Don't give the person the opportunity to start a disagreement. Stay in direct contact with God, Jesus, and His Holy Spirit. Allow them to have full control of your life, your thoughts, and your words. Be prepared through studying His Word and praying regularly. You can talk to God all the time, because His Spirit lives within you and knows your every thought.

> *For this reason we also, since the day we heard it, do not cease to pray for you, and to ask that you may be filled with the knowledge of His will in all wisdom and spiritual understanding.* (Colossians 1:9)

> *Those who live only to satisfy their own sinful nature will harvest decay and death from that sinful nature. But those who live to please the Spirit will harvest everlasting life from the Spirit.* (Galatians 6:8 NLT)

> *And because you are sons, God has sent forth the Spirit of His Son into your hearts, crying out, "Abba, Father!"* (Galatians 4:6)

Chapter 17

CODEPENDENCY

Codependency is a major problem. Often, it is a hidden relationship dysfunction that develops out of love but soon turns into fear. One spouse loves the other spouse so much; they work hard to actively cover over, or hide, all the faults, mistakes, and misbehaviors of the other spouse. No one wants to admit they made a mistake by marrying someone with hidden issues, however, many of these dysfunctional behaviors don't manifest until months or years after the vows have been made.

Even though codependency often develops with a habitual behavior, such as excessive drinking, drug use, abuse (verbal, physical, sexual, or mental), its signs and symptoms can pop up in almost every relationship. Whether those signs develop into a serious codependent situation depends on the awareness and recognition of the unhealthy relationship.

Narcissistic behavior is a commonly identified issue. One of two people involved is concerned mainly with "self." Every action, spoken word, attitude, or behavior is centered on their personal desires. This person might have experienced abandonment as a child or as an adult. Perhaps there was only one parent in the family and many children to nurture. Parents who are away from home working long hours also can affect the child's development. Jealousy as a child or an adult can also breed this dysfunctional behavior.

You may hear them say, "I will never allow this or that to happen again." They take control and won't allow anybody else to express an opinion. Their history often paints the picture of extreme loneliness and anger during their emotional development.

The codependent party always wants to fix the situation, keep the other spouse happy, and is compliant to their desires. It is a "no win" situation. No one can please another person 100 percent of the time. Erratic behavior cannot be soothed easily. The "narcissist" will manipulate the other when away from their support system of friends and family. This includes anyone who could encourage the codependent to separate from the unhealthy relationship. Going to a counselor wouldn't be received well, because a mistake or misbehavior would come to light. The narcissist doesn't accept guilt because they believe they are always right.

Often, codependence begins in childhood. A young child develops an excessive reliance on other people, such as a parent, for approval. A child's sense of identity can be totally wrapped up in a parent who clings to the child and won't allow independent behavior or healthy self-development. It sounds like smothering love, but it goes beyond that. Some areas of growth are actually hindered by emotional abandonment, manipulation, withholding, or other uncaring behavior.

If the strong personality realizes what they are doing, they may enjoy being in control of the relationship. The weaker party works hard to please and meet excessive demands. It may begin by pleasing the parent in all things, then it may move on to teachers, friends, and finally, a spouse. Emotions of the codependent are under the control and whim of the stronger narcissistic partner.

Some people identify strongly with their job or occupation. Without that, they fall apart. Others may sympathize so strongly with a sick friend that they develop the same disease symptoms. If a person feels so neglected and abandoned, they may sleep with everyone and anyone just to feel wanted by someone. If a man is hurt deeply by a woman, he may turn to another man. Conversely, when a woman is seriously hurt by a man, especially at a young age, she may be more receptive to a woman's love than a man's.

A friend of mine was unable to ever say "no." Pleasing others was very important to her. She would climb out of bed in the middle of the night to help someone in need. She took on more assignments than was healthy for her wellbeing. Her desires, needs, and wants were always secondary, or last, on the list. Until she recognized what was happening, she couldn't become the independent person God wanted her to be.

No one wants to admit this kind of dysfunction. Recognizing what it is and recovering from it takes time and great wisdom. Few people will freely admit their symptoms. They will find excuses for their actions until God opens their eyes to the truth.

People trapped in this kind of relationship lose much of their own identity and life. Subtle symptoms can often be easily recognized by a recovering codependent. I say "recovering," because the behavior is easy to fall back into. Just like an alcoholic has to stay away from any and all alcohol, the codependent must stay away from that relationship that can draw them back into excessive dependence on another person.

Often, the behavior can be identified as someone goes from relationship to relationship, or marriage to marriage, in which the same old problems keep popping up repeatedly. Women are often the codependent party to a strong-willed male; however, men can also have the same issues.

THOSE MOST SUSCEPTIBLE TO CODEPENDENCY
ARE THE CAREGIVERS OF THE WORLD. THEY WANT
TO TAKE CARE OF, NURTURE, AND DELIVER THE
SOLUTION TO EVERYONE ELSE'S PROBLEMS. HIGH
ON THE LIST ARE WOMEN WHO ARE NATURALLY
NURTURERS, NURSES WHO CARE FOR THE
HELPLESS AND INFIRM, AND CHRISTIANS. EACH
HAS TO LEARN WHEN TO BACK OFF AND ALLOW
THE OTHER PERSON TO HANDLE THEIR OWN ISSUES
AND MAKE THEIR OWN DECISIONS.

Those most susceptible to codependency are the caregivers of the world. They want to take care of, nurture, and deliver the solution to everyone else's problems. High on the list are women who are naturally nurturers, nurses who care for the helpless and infirm, and Christians. Each has to learn when to back off and allow the other person to handle their own issues and make their own decisions. This is often called "cutting the apron strings," or I have also heard "cut the umbilical cord." They both mean the same thing. Let them go. Let them be independent of you. They need to stand on their own two feet. They have to learn to depend on God.

God is the only One you should be concerned about obeying and pleasing 100 percent of the time. He is the only One with your best interests in mind every day and every minute. Please Him. Teach others to do the same thing. Don't depend on man. Depend on Him! Be codependent on your heavenly Father!

A lady came to me for prayer for her marriage of over twenty years. This was her second marriage. She had three daughters by her first husband. She explained that her current spouse had molested all three of her daughters. As could be expected, this abhorrent behavior had caused all kinds of problems with the children, including anger, distrust, frustration, and pain. Now grown and developing their own families, the children had forgiven her for not protecting them, stopping the behaviors, and not getting justice for them.

She added, "He continues to sleep around. He considers this an open marriage."

The woman knew what he was doing. She didn't approve of, or want, an "open marriage."

"Why are you staying with him?" I inquired.

"Money," she answered.

"You essentially gave him permission to steal the innocence of your daughters. You are now allowing him to make further

IN EVERY RELATIONSHIP, THERE IS A DANGER OF CODEPENDENCY! IT IS A SECRET, SUBTLE SICKNESS, LIKE A CANCER THAT SLOWLY BUT SURELY KILLS FROM WITHIN.

ungodly covenants with all these other women. He still wants to come home and have an intimate relationship with you also. This opens up the doors for all kinds of diseases to come to you," I explained.

She had been trapped in this situation for a long time. I knew I had to shock her into reality. I said, "You are doing this just for money? That makes you a prostitute!"

During my years of codependency, I knew I couldn't make it financially without my first husband, but I couldn't live in that kind of situation any longer. I had to separate myself and the girls from a father who was entrenched in a continuous, ungodly lifestyle.

Am I promoting divorce? No, but I personally had to establish boundaries. I had to protect myself and my children. I knew I had a call of God on my life and I couldn't compromise that assignment. I had to say, "You are not going to do this to me or my family anymore. You either change or do something about this." He wouldn't change. We got a divorce.

In every relationship, there is a danger of codependency! It is a secret, subtle sickness, like a cancer that slowly but surely kills from within. I had to take a stand. It was not easy. I was filled with fear and hopelessness at the time. My life was wrapped up in my relationship with my spouse of twenty-five years. I didn't realize codependency was a sickness.

Believe me when I say, I am *no proponent* of divorce!

If you recognize these symptoms have crept into your marriage, seek God first. If possible, seek marriage counseling. Denial of any codependent behaviors is common, but don't give up. Usually, the two parties involved have to separate themselves from this unhealthy situation. I cried out to God because I knew I couldn't do this on my own.

God was waiting in the wings of my life. He knew what was going on, but He could only wait until I was ready to listen. I threw

WHEN ONE SPOUSE MAKES ALL THE DECISIONS
IN A RELATIONSHIP, KNOWS AND MANAGES ALL
THE FINANCES, AN UNHEALTHY DEPENDENCY
DEVELOPS. THE SURVIVING PARTY FINDS
THEMSELF COMPLETELY HELPLESS AND
UNABLE TO MAKE EVEN THE SMALLEST DECISION.
THEY REACT LIKE A SMALL CHILD LOST IN A
CONFUSING WORLD.

myself into His lap and accepted all He could give me. He took care of me, my daughters, and my needs better than I ever could have. He was so faithful to develop my potential from a quiet, behind the scenes servant to the head of an international ministry with my own TV show. I really came out from behind the scenes and onto God's worldwide stage, where I can proclaim His story to the four corners of the earth.

SEVERE DEPENDENCY

There are some people who have made a vow (or covenant) with death. For instance, they say, "I will die if something happens to my wife (or husband)" or "I can't live without you!" When someone does die, the survivor can experience a "broken heart syndrome," which I discussed earlier. This happens because they feel there is nothing left to live for. This is more common when the couple is in their later years and the aging body can't survive such a traumatic event.

A severe dependency can affect life in nearly the same way. If something happens to a spouse, can the other survive alone? When one spouse makes all the decisions in a relationship, knows and manages all the finances, an unhealthy dependency develops. The surviving party finds themself completely helpless and unable to make even the smallest decision. They react like a small child lost in a confusing world.

This situation is understandable when there is a medical condition or mental deficiency that requires custodial supervision and management. However, when this develops from a controlling spirit, the outcome can be devastating. In a marriage partnership, both parties should be equally involved with decision making within the relationship.

I recently heard about a couple who demonstrated this severe dependency. The husband is seriously dependent on his wife. He barely can breathe without her telling him what to do. When she had to go away for a few days to attend a family celebration, he didn't know what to do. He felt totally lost. What should he eat? What TV program should he watch? Should he answer the doorbell? This is sad.

What if one was hospitalized for a long period of time in a coma? If the other cannot make a decision, what a mess will develop. When the sick partner recovers, their life together could be destroyed from mismanagement.

Total dependence on another person is unhealthy. Unless there is a medical or mental deficiency that requires a health surrogate or power of attorney, such a relationship needs to be reevaluated. Children should be taught to make decisions early in life. Relinquishing that basic right is wrong. Make sure your partner can take care of themselves independently of you.

This gentleman was far too dependent on his wife. A family member explained, "He would starve himself to death if anything ever happened to her." Physically, he would struggle to survive without her.

I pray this experience showed his family what needs to be done to correct the situation before it's too late. There was no dependency on alcohol or drugs in this case, just an unhealthy codependency.

WHEN IS ENOUGH ENOUGH?

Each person must answer this question for themselves. I believe the goal for every relationship is to help the other person become the best they can be. Sometimes, God brings two people together for a lifetime friendship, some you meet only in passing. Some make perfect friends, others may become a confidante. Only that special one person should become a spouse for a forever relationship. It is so vital to pray and seek God for instruction as to who you will be physically, emotionally, financially, and mentally attached to for life. God will take control and guide you to that special person.

Unfortunately, love is often blind. Outside appearances or behaviors often camouflage what is hidden within. It is vital to communicate in every area of life in order to walk together in God-directed unity. Somewhere along the path of marital bliss, the bumps appear. What bumps did you discover? Have you discussed them? Are both parties willing to discuss differences of opinion or behavior? When is enough enough?

Abuse occurs in many forms: physical, mental, emotional, sexual, or financial. Hopefully, counseling with a pastor or professional counselor will ease the difficulty and resume unity. Realistically, many can't or won't accept outside advice from anyone. If you are faced with any kind of abuse, you need to remove yourself immediately! If any children are being injured, you must get them to safety immediately! There are many safe havens available! Find one!

Everyone's safety is paramount. A restraining order can be obtained to legally keep the perpetrator away from you; however, this doesn't solve the underlying problem. Ask your Christian friends, seek assistance from your church or pastor. Someone will be able to advise you on the next step to take.

Often, alcohol or drugs worm their way into a situation. These mind-altering substances usually cause destruction behind their usage. People believe life is better under their influences, and it draws them into a life-altering addiction or dependence. Decision-making is corrupted and abnormal behaviors quickly follow.

A Christian man who had a wonderful wife went on an important business trip. As is usual, the hosts offered alcoholic beverages at an open bar. After indulging in a few drinks, the man's senses were dulled and inhibitions erased. He woke up the

ABUSE OCCURS IN MANY FORMS: PHYSICAL, MENTAL, EMOTIONAL, SEXUAL, OR FINANCIAL....
IF YOU ARE FACED WITH ANY KIND OF ABUSE, YOU NEED TO REMOVE YOURSELF IMMEDIATELY!
IF ANY CHILDREN ARE BEING INJURED, YOU MUST GET THEM TO SAFETY IMMEDIATELY! THERE ARE MANY SAFE HAVENS AVAILABLE! FIND ONE!

next morning and learned that he had gone to a hotel room with a stranger and had a sexual encounter. He didn't remember all the details and quickly blamed his misbehavior on the alcohol. In part, he was correct. The alcohol blurred the truth, hid any common sense that normally governed his actions, and caused him to lie to his wife and employer.

Decisions made under the influence of drugs or alcohol rarely resemble sober decisions made with intact memory and faculties. Most believe just one or two drinks have no effect on their behavior. Unfortunately, they don't see or hear what they do under the influence. Accidents, injuries, rape, and all types of abuse are often precipitated by mind-altering substances.

It comes down to a quality decision. Do you want to be in control of your life or allow the enemy to take control through these substances that take over your mind and control your actions? Who do you want to control your life? God or the enemy?

Throughout every step you take, keep God in the forefront! The Holy Spirit will guide you. Listen for His voice and obey. God will take care of you. He has someone waiting just for you! Follow peace! Fear is from the enemy who is after you, your partner, and your family. He wants to destroy your future, your destiny, and your legacy through your children.

Endeavor to always please God, not man! Stand as His child, with His strength flowing through your veins. Put on His armor and resist the enemy! Realize that the enemy is Satan, not your partner! Give your partner to God and let Him handle the changes that need to be made. Arguing and fighting won't accomplish anything but more stress, trauma, and pain.

EMOTIONAL COVENANT

I must add another factor to this discussion. Even though codependency is usually identified within a marriage, it can also develop between two people who are not married. For instance, through relationships of a parent/child, a teacher/student, an employee/employer, or just between close friends. This could also be described as an "emotional covenant," a relationship without the sexual component. Some may call this a soul tie, which is not scriptural.

Is your happiness or self-confidence rooted in another person's behavior? Do you seek someone's approval for every plan or action you take? Does their disapproval throw you into depression, despondent and feeling like an utter failure?

The believer's true joy and happiness is based in Jesus alone. Man is fickle, and emotions are often erratic and undependable. But God is always the same. He never changes. He will always instruct you to do what is the best for you. He will not play you like a puppet, while He laughs at your stupidity, as the enemy does.

It seems that every family has that one person who irritates, pecks at, and causes no end of trauma or turmoil within the family unit. Realize that the enemy will attempt to creep into the family to sow dissension and chaos. He knows the power in two or more of God's children working together. The enemy never stops His tactics. Stand with God's purpose foremost in your heart and mind.

If physical separation becomes necessary, know that God will take care of you. Stand with His arms of protection around you. Walk in His footsteps, because He will guide you into a healthy, loving, and joy-filled relationship. Your future is bright and golden. Grab His promises and put codependency behind you. Know that you will be able to help the next person who feels like they are trapped in a similar situation. Speak freedom and peace, and then walk into it with your eyes wide open to His understanding and wisdom!

Chapter 18

GOD LIVES WITHIN YOU

Don't tear down another person with your words. Instead, keep the peace, and be considerate. Be truly humble toward everyone because there was a time when we, too, were foolish, rebellious, and deceived—we were slaves to sensual cravings and pleasures; and we spent our lives being spiteful, envious, hated by many, and hating one another. But then something happened: God our Savior and His overpowering love and kindness for humankind entered our world; He came to save us. It's not that we earned it by doing good works or righteous deeds; He came because He is merciful. He brought us out of our old ways of living to a new beginning through the washing of regeneration; and He made us completely new through the Holy Spirit, who was poured out in abundance through Jesus the Anointed, our Savior. All of this happened so that through His grace we would be accepted into God's covenant family and appointed to be His heirs, full of the hope that comes from knowing you have eternal life. This is a faithful statement of what we believe.

Concerning this, I want you to put it out there boldly so that those who believe in God will be constant in doing the right things, which will benefit all of us.   (Titus 3:2–8 VOICE)

What relationships do you desire to strengthen? Your relationship with your spouse? Your friend? How about with God? Do you want a close, intimate relationship with your heavenly Father, His Spirit, and His precious Son, Jesus?

When you wanted to get closer to your spouse or a new friend, you spent more quality time with them. You may have to do that again and again. You will have to make a quality decision to do that same thing to improve your relationship with God. Spend quiet time with Him, study His Word, talk to Him frequently, and, most importantly, listen to Him.

Listen to teaching by respected men of God on TV, radio, or online. Read highly recommended books about God and His Word. You will find that as you read and learn more about Him, you will also learn much about yourself.

Allow His Words to change you, to mold you into what He designed you to become. True happiness and peace is found when you are in the center of His will for your life. Pray this prayer:

Father, I want an intimate relationship with You on a daily, even minute by minute basis. Forgive me for getting distracted by other worldly things. Forgive me if I have ever blamed you for something that I felt was wrong, because You always do good things for me. Your plans are perfect.

Keep me close to Your heart, Father. Don't let me stray away from Your path. Guide me, protect me and love me. Thank You for Your unlimited blessings and unconditional love. In Jesus' name. Amen.

At your salvation, you invited Jesus to live within you. How is your relationship with Him today? Do you honor Him and thank Him for all He does for you? Do you worship Him as Lord of your life and King of all Kings?

Worship Him, Praise Him, Love on Him, and Thank Him. He is your Lord forever. Share His story with others! Reach out and touch another hurting soul and introduce them to Jesus!

Whatever you do, He does with you! When you reach out in love, He touches others through you. When I minister healing to the sick, I know Jesus is touching and healing through me. I, Joan, can't heal anyone, but Jesus working through me certainly can! He is my Healer, my Savior, my Joy, and my Peace. I love Him so much!

When I speak, Jesus speaks through me. Where I walk, He walks with me. He will never leave me! I will never, ever be alone again! What an amazing gift from my Father!

Then He who sat on the throne said, "Behold, I make all things new."   (Revelation 21:5)

The Lord wants to restore your heart and body. Restoring your body to purity also includes your virginity. Jesus made the way for you to be pure in heart, soul, and body. Follow His instructions. Become a new creation.

MY INTERVIEW WITH MATT AND STEPHANIE SORGER

TO REMAIN PURE...

When I got married, I was a virgin. I didn't bring anything but purity into my first marriage. On the other hand, my spouse had not been celibate and brought much junk into the marriage. Back then, I didn't understand covenant relationship responsibilities, and the spiritual damage that eventually affected our union.

Recently, I interviewed Matt and Stephanie Sorger when they came to minister at Four Corners Conference Center. I knew I had to include their testimony for you. Matt Sorger is an international speaker and author who has ministered in over thirty-five countries. He is a preacher, teacher, and prophet, specializing in healing the body of Christ. He has been both a host of his own TV show as well as a guest on numerous national and international TV shows of well-known ministers across the country. Stephanie Sorger is a creative writer, philanthropist, and speaker, who travels full time with her husband. Together, they founded Rescue1, a mercy mission to free women and children trapped in sex trafficking in India, China, Philippines, and Africa.

Together they are an explosive and blessed duo working for the Lord wherever they go.

When Matt first started traveling, he never went anywhere without his dad. They went everywhere together. Nobody was ever given the opportunity to get close enough to entice Matt into compromising his values and convictions to stay sexually pure for his future marriage.

MATT:

A successful marriage happens when two whole people come together and being able to give 100 percent of themselves to each other. This is the basis for a successful and healthy marriage.

Years ago, I learned that Billy Graham never traveled alone. That made a positive impression on me. My dad and I set this same policy in place early in my ministry. While I was single in ministry, my dad was my travel partner for fourteen years. He always had my back. He was my covering, security, and accountability partner. I had my own personal conviction and rules, but having Dad with me gave me extra levels of protection and boundaries.

Stephanie and I got married when I was forty years old. Yes, I was a forty-year-old virgin. Of course, when I got married, Stephanie became my permanent travel partner.

JOAN:

In worldly terms, being a virgin seems stupid and ridiculous. In God's world, this is absolutely perfect. He wants this relationship to remain pure. Today's society claims sleeping around is normal and acceptable. Following the world's standards, a person leaves part of their heart and soul scattered amongst all their sexual partners of the past. To later attempt to gather all those pieces together is sometimes difficult.

Do you realize how rare you two are?

MATT:

Before we got married, we went to a doctor for the required blood tests. The doctor was shocked and pleased when he discovered we both were virgins. During his professional career, he could only recall three people who were still virgins at our age.

JOAN:

It is rare to find anyone, let alone a male at age forty, who is still a virgin. You *both* were. This will bring hope to so many people. They can wait until marriage. They can stay pure, as God desires. Through the years, you knew Stephanie was waiting but you had no idea when or where. Your thoughts remained pure. You had that barrier to protect you, and you maintained that boundary. God shielded your eyes and protected you. Then, you two met in Mozambique, where you were ministering with Heidi Baker, both doing exactly what God told you to do. Walking in obedience halfway around the world, God brought you together.

Your dad gave Stephanie your ministry contact business card and asked her to stay in touch. He was watching your back while watching out for your future relationships and marriage.

MATT:

When I was saved at fourteen, I had the benefit of finding God at such a young age. I had a strong, sensitive conscience toward God. I knew that if I was to please God, I would have to live in a way that pleased Him. As a teenager, I had a strong relationship with Him.

Many people endure their teenage years and complain about their single years. They are always looking forward to the future. They don't believe they will be happy until they are married. A person doesn't have to wait for marriage to be happy.

I chose to maximize my relationship with God. I spent many hours in prayer and in His Word. This prepared me for ministry, as well as for marriage. I made sure I had practical, healthy boundaries in place, as well as convictions to preserve purity. For instance, I would never be alone in a room with a woman.

As a Christian spending time in the dating arena, or developing a relationship with a potential husband or wife, those boundaries must be maintained. Knowing the necessary boundaries to put in place is very important. Keep purity intact until marriage.

Maximize your single years in preparation for what God has for your future. Your relationship with God will keep you pure.

STEPHANIE:

From the standpoint of a woman, when speaking about sexual purity, knowing your value and worth in God is key to remain pure. We are bombarded by images of what we are to be, what we are to give away, and how we are to obtain love from a man.

God calls us to be His precious daughter—pure and holy. You are loved by God. A woman doesn't have to pursue love from a man in a sexual way in order to have identity, validation, and acceptance. That love first comes freely from the Father. Women, know your identify as a daughter of God. Stay sexually pure for your spouse. Give him that precious gift reserved for marriage.

JOAN:

You two are an exceptional example to the body of Christ. Virginity at age twenty-one is rare, but at age forty, it is extremely rare, amazing, and a miracle.

MATT:

God's grace kept us. It can also keep others who are waiting to find that perfect mate. Set boundaries and keep them in place. Virginity is a special gift you give only to your spouse. However, if you have already given that precious gift away, there is still restoration in God. There is healing. God can make you pure and clean again. God's grace is also there to help you set boundaries to protect your future.

~

It is possible and acceptable to remain sexually pure until your wedding day. In fact, it is God's plan. If you aren't a virgin, God can restore you to the virgin attitude of health and wholeness.

> *"Come now, let's settle this," says the Lord. "Though your sins are like scarlet, I will make them as white as snow. Though they are red like crimson, I will make them as white as wool.*
>
> (Isaiah 1:18)

Make the quality decision right now. Determine to set your heart after God. His arms are open wide to receive you. You don't have to clean yourself up. He knows everything you have done in the past and He still has a marvelous plan for your life. He can and will make you totally new. You may even wonder, *Who was that person I used to be?*

Turn your eyes on Him and give Him your wounded and shattered heart. He is an expert at mending broken hearts. Accept His peace, love, and joy!

> *For I know the plans I have for you," says the Lord. "They are plans for good and not for disaster, to give you a future and a hope.* (Jeremiah 29:11 NLT)

Just in case you haven't asked Jesus into your life yet, consider it seriously. He is everything. You don't have to do anything fancy or difficult. Just repeat this prayer:

> Jesus, I want You in my life. Please forgive me for my sins. I repent and turn my back on the way I have been living. I welcome You into my heart right now. Make me new! Guide my footsteps from this day forward. Live within me. Thank You, Jesus! Amen.

Has anyone else ever died for your mistakes? Has anyone paid the price for a new life? Has anyone opened the door to heaven and eternal life for you? If you said that prayer, you can say a resounding, "yes!" Jesus did all that for you and more! Love on Him, and allow Him to be your best Friend forever.

> *For you were once darkness, but now you are light in the Lord. Walk as children of light (for the fruit of the Spirit is in all goodness, righteousness, and truth), finding out what is acceptable to the Lord.* (Ephesians 5:8–10)

> *For there are three that bear witness in heaven: the Father, the Word, and the Holy Spirit; and these three are one.* (1 John 5:7)

> *Or do you not know that your body is the temple of the Holy Spirit who is in you, whom you have from God, and you are not your own?* (1 Corinthians 6:19)

And now, dear brothers and sisters, one final thing. Fix your thoughts on what is true, and honorable, and right, and pure, and lovely, and admirable. Think about things that are excellent and worthy of praise. (Philippians 4:8 NLT)

When Jesus enters your life, He also brings the Holy Spirit as a Mentor, Counselor, and Friend. The Holy Spirit is like having an encyclopedia of pure wisdom and truth ready and waiting for you at any hour of the day. When you have a question, just ask. The Holy Spirit is waiting to serve you and help you.

To hear Him, however, you may have to practice being quiet for a while. In contrast, you may need to pray using His heavenly language that only God understands. Praying in tongues can be silent, normal, or loud. He always hears you.

The Holy Spirit always directs you toward Jesus, never away from Him. He doesn't need or want your worship, which is reserved for Jesus and the Father. The Holy Spirit is always ready to answer your questions, guide you, and teach you what you are to do next. Call on Him. He is waiting to help you live and produce the Fruit of the Spirit.

But the fruit of the Spirit is love, joy, peace, longsuffering, kindness, goodness, faithfulness, gentleness, self-control. Against such there is no law. (Galatians 5:22–23)

You were cleansed from your sins when you obeyed the truth, so now you must show sincere love to each other as brothers and sisters. Love each other deeply with all your heart. (1 Peter 1:22 NLT)

Father, I have Your Son, Jesus, living within my heart. I also know that I need Your blessed Holy Spirit to help me and teach me what to do and where to go. I give You my voice to pray perfectly to you in a language only You understand. Let me speak, pray, and sing to You, Father. I love You. I thank You, Jesus, for all You have done for me. Now, let me do my best to serve You in every area of my life!

Thank You for the revelation of how to love again and live again, Father. Guide me as I reconnect with others and walk in Your path of love and understanding. Help me share Your message of reconciliation with others, as I walk with You. Take my whole heart, Father. I freely give it all to You. I know You are the Healer, Father. You make all things new. Father, I want to be white as snow in Your eyes. Renew my heart. Renew my virginity. Allow me to be whole again, Father, so I can give my whole heart and body to the one You have planned to be my partner and spouse forever. In Jesus's name. Amen.

Look forward to great relationships....both with God and your fellow man.

ABOUT THE AUTHOR

Joan Hunter is a compassionate minister, dynamic teacher, accomplished author, and anointed healing evangelist who has devoted her life to carry a message of hope, deliverance, and healing to the nations. As founder and president of Joan Hunter Ministries, Hearts 4 Him, and 4 Corners Foundation, and president of Hunter Ministries, Joan has a vision to equip believers to take the healing power of God "beyond the four walls of the church to the four corners of the earth." Joan's genuine approach and candid delivery enables her to connect intimately with people from all walks of life. Some describe her as "Carol Burnett with the anointing of Jesus."

Joan ministers the gospel with manifestations of supernatural signs and wonders in healing schools, miracle services, conferences, churches, and revival centers around the world. She is sensitive to the move of the Spirit and speaks prophetically to the local body and into the individual lives of those in attendance. Joan's genuine approach and candid delivery enable her to connect intimately with people from all educational, social, and cultural backgrounds.

At the tender age of twelve, Joan committed her life to Christ and began faithfully serving in ministry alongside her parents, Charles and Frances Hunter, as they traveled around the globe conducting Healing Explosions and Healing Schools until their deaths. Prior to branching out into her own international healing ministry, Joan also co-pastored a church for eighteen years.

Joan brings a powerful ministry to a world characterized by brokenness and pain. Having emerged victorious through tragic circumstances, impossible obstacles, and immeasurable devastation, Joan is able to share a message of hope and restoration to the brokenhearted, deliverance and freedom to the bound, and healing and wholeness to the diseased. Joan's life is one of uncompromising dedication to the gospel of Jesus Christ, as she exhibits a sincere desire to see the body of Christ live in freedom, happiness, wholeness, and financial wellness.

Joan has ministered in countries all over the world and has been featured on Sid Roth's *It's Supernatural, My New Day* with Drs. Bob and Audrey Meisner, *Everlasting Love* with Patricia King, and on Marilyn Hickey's *Today with Marilyn and Sarah.* Joan hosts a powerful and exciting show of her own, *Miracles Happen!* Joan's television appearances have been broadcast around the world on World Harvest Network, Inspiration Network, Daystar, Faith TV, Cornerstone TV, The Church Channel, Total Christian Television, Christian Television Network, Watchmen Broadcasting, and God TV.

She is a noted author whose books include *Healing the Whole Man Handbook, Healing the Heart, Power to Heal, Supernatural Provision, Freedom Beyond Comprehension,* and *Miracle Maintenance.*

Joan and her husband, Kelley, live northwest of Houston, Texas. Together, they have four daughters, four sons, three sons-in-law, and seven grandchildren.

Welcome to Our House!

We Have a Special Gift for You

It is our privilege and pleasure to share in your love of Christian books. We are committed to bringing you authors and books that feed, challenge, and enrich your faith.

To show our appreciation, we invite you to sign up to receive a specially selected **Reader Appreciation Gift**, with our compliments. Just go to the Web address at the bottom of this page.

God bless you as you seek a deeper walk with Him!

WE HAVE A GIFT FOR YOU. VISIT:

whpub.me/nonfictionthx

WHITAKER
HOUSE